M000279728

UNTETHERED

UNTETHERED

A Woman's Search for Self
on the Edge of India

A Travel Memoir

C.L. STAMBUSH

UNTETHERED © 2021 by C.L. Stambush

All rights reserved. No part of this book may be reproduced in any form or by any electronic or mechanical means, including information storage and retrieval systems, without permission in writing from the author, except by reviewers, who may quote brief passages in a review. Please purchase only authorized electronic editions, and do not participate in or encourage electronic piracy of copyrighted materials. Your support of the author's rights is appreciated.

ISBN: 978-1-7362541-1-0 (Print)
ISBN: 978-1-7362541-0-3 (eBook)

Library of Congress Control Number: 2021900555

Cover design and map by Terri Bischoff

First Edition Print February 2021
Printed in United States of America

hello@clstambush.com
www.clstambush.com

Dedication

For my mother who taught me to be me every day.
For my father who said what I needed to hear.
For all goddesses who long to go, do, be.

Author's Note

This book was created based on my journals, my memory, and research. The quotes, while not verbatim, represent real conversations. The people in this book are real. I have changed the names of many but not all the people to preserve their privacy. Memory is malleable and my journals don't capture every moment of the trip, but I have remained true to the facts to the best of my ability while creating this story.

Map of Journey

C.L. Stambush's
journey around
India

Through the Looking Glass

1

The Urge

I heard the crowd of agitated men shouting at me, "Leave it." The man I was after turned to look back before he hopped over the Nehru Bridge wall and dropped into the dark alley below. I followed him, flinging myself over as he did, hitting the ground hard. His footfalls echoed ahead of me in the night, and I spotted flashes of his shirt flitting as I ran after him. Adrenaline pumped my blood, sounding like a locomotive in my ears, as one thought drove me: Get him.

I was gaining on him when my foot snagged on a root, hurling me to my hands and knees, and knocking the breath out of me.

Stunned and shattered, I crouched quivering in the alley as my breath and senses slowly returned. In the muggy subcontinent air, ripe with the stench of rotten fruit and piss, I prayed for the earth to swallow me. Prayed the Hindu goddesses would pity me enough for this to be a nightmare. But the taste of blood in my mouth from biting my tongue and the scrapes on the palms of my hands told me it was real. Unable to move, I sat there wondering, *What had I done? Who had I become?*

This was not me. Not the me I'd hoped to discover when I bought a Royal Enfield Bullet motorcycle and set out to ride it solo on the edge of India. Three months earlier I'd been sitting in an office at the Women's Feature Service, a news agency in New Delhi, India, complaining to a fellow editor, Patralekha, about a 3,000-word story a writer sent instead of the 800 I'd assigned. The adventurous life I'd come in search of two years earlier had morphed into a routine, sedate, predictable life, filled with 8-to-5 work, shopping on weekends, and hanging out with friends.

My contract as one of three editors with the agency was ending, awakening a familiar desire to test my grit, and I'd bought a Bullet. When I shared my plan with coworkers, they didn't cheer "you-go-girl" as I'd expected. (We were, after all, a women's empowerment news agency.) The office manager Mrs. Banerjee listened with the primness of a Persian cat before issuing a dismissive "preposterous" head shake. My co-editor Patralekha said nothing, but her eyes widened in alarm as if to say, *ARE YOU CRAZY?*

Given the facts I'd read in a government report, stating only thirty-six percent of India's drivers were aware of safety rules, twenty-seven percent understood traffic signals, signs and markings, fifty-five percent disregarded flashing signals, twenty-five percent ignored speed limits, twenty-eight percent refrained from using hand signals (most vehicles didn't have functioning electrical ones), and thirty-three percent displayed a frightening "propensity for abrupt lane changes," I understood their concerns.

Two million miles of road—paved and unpaved—crisscrossed India in 1997, making it the third largest road network in the world after the United States and China. Yet, only two percent of the roads were national highways, carrying forty percent of the traffic and accounting for twenty-five percent of all accidents. Trucks and busses comprised seven percent of vehicles but were responsible for forty-three percent of accidents. Untrained, stoned and drunk truckers ruled the roads, and they rarely gave an inch to anyone.

Those who didn't think I was crazy called me courageous, but I considered it a compulsion. As a first grader in school I slid my shoulder along the hall wall—even when I was alone—afraid to detach myself for fear something bad would happen. Nothing ever did, but this memory of myself, as someone afraid of life, had become lodged in me and puckered like a scar that I'd worried my fingers over for years. It restricted me, defined me as incapable, and kept me on life's sidelines. It was only in the black-and-white glow of Westerns I watched on television as a kid, while sopping up cold beans with a slice of bread, that I escaped how I thought of myself by pretending I was one of the rough riders free on the range.

Despite thirty-seven years of trying to prove to myself I'd become the woman I wanted to be—one who moved confidently through life, who owned the space she occupied, who felt capable in a world that suggested women were not—the essence of that timid girl still clung to part of me. This journey was a last chance to prove to myself that I was no longer that girl, and the Royal Enfield Bullet—a modern-day iron horse—was the perfect vehicle to set me free.

The simplest and easiest route was to ride along India's coast. But it felt uninspired and I'd lamented this to Patralekha.

"Why don't you seek out the shakti peetha temples?" she'd said, "They are dedicated to the goddess Kali you've named your motorcycle after."

I'd never named any of the seven cars I'd owned, but the thought of being out there alone—disconnected from the familiar and my sense of place—stirred a desire for a companion. In naming my motorcycle Kali, I'd intuitively concocted a particular partner, knowing a woman alone sometimes needed a little venom. The goddess Kali had more than a smidgen to offer. With her wild hair, lolling red tongue, and flashing black eyes, she represents destruction and rebirth in Hinduism. To believers, she bestows energy, strength, and capability. A warrior with four arms, she wears the severed limbs of her enemies as a skirt and their shrunken heads around her neck like pearls. She is the quintessential badass, and I wanted her grrrr.

The shakti peetha temples' origins are in the legend of the goddess Sati who immolated her mortal body when her father refused to welcome her husband Shiva into the family. Upon her death, the grief-stricken Shiva began a dance of destruction and Lord Vishnu, fearing the ruin of the newly formed Earth, cut Sati's body into fifty-one pieces to stop Shiva's dance.

Sati is a manifestation of Kali, The Mother Goddess, and one of thirty-six million Hindu deities. The shakti peetha temples—symbolizing where her lips, eyes, nose, ears, heart, and so on, fell to Earth, transforming the locations into sacred empowerment sites—are also known as Kali temples. For centuries, pilgrims have trekked to the temples to pay homage to the goddess, seeking her help in shedding their old selves to become the person they're meant to be.

I'm not religious or spiritual, but the idea of finding temples and metaphorically reassembling the goddess appealed to me. I'd never attempted such an arduous adventure and finding the temples gave me structure, providing, if nothing else, mile markers in my quest to define myself.

Patralekha gave me a map indicating the temples' locations a few days later. I carefully unfolded it, smoothing out the creases. It didn't have the red road lines or blue, brown, and green shadings of most maps, rather it was a simple outline of India annotated with Xs, representing the location of each shakti peetha temple. Scanning the map, I noticed the temples dotted the edge of India, echoing my inclination to ride the coast, and my plan slid into place.

2

The Quest

India is massive and complicated: culturally, psychologically, ethnically, and physically. Despite its landmass being one-third the size of the United States, it's the second largest country in Asia, after China, and the seventh largest in the world. From north to south—Kashmir to Tamil Nadu—India stretches 1,997 miles. From west to east—Rajasthan to West Bengal—it spans another 1,882. Seventeen states and 8,763 miles root northern India to the Asian continent, connecting it to Pakistan, China, Nepal, Bangladesh, Bhutan, and Myanmar. The remaining 4,671 miles of coastal India bite into the salty waters of the Arabian Sea, the Lakshadweep Sea, the Indian Ocean, the Gulf of Mannar, and the Bay of Bengal like a tiger's tooth, tapering to a single point you can practically stand on.

The long, northern snowy sweep of the Himalayans and its hundreds of frozen peaks functioned as a line of protection against invaders, a defense historically breached by outsiders. For thousands of years, India swallowed her marauders, absorbing their religions and cultures into what has become a throbbing mass of diversity, where more than 19,000 different languages are spoken, twenty-two of them official Indian languages, and thirteen sanctioned written scripts. Luckily, English is widely spoken, and although I'd studied Hindi at a school in the Himalayan foothills as part of my journey's preparation, I didn't need to attempt using it when I bought my Royal Enfield Bullet.

The motorcycle dealers were in Old Delhi, past the sandstone arches of Kashmir Gate and down among the warren of dealers specializing in gold, silver, spices, sweets, carpets, perfumes, silk, books, shawls, shoes, oils, and more. Two months before my contract with the news service ended, I clambered into a rickshaw with a friend and neighbor Thomas to buy an Enfield. He'd ridden motorcycles all his life and owned a Bullet, while my only riding experience was a one-week training course in an empty parking lot a month earlier while visiting friends and family in the United States. During the course, I popped a wheelie and crashed, banging my knee and terrifying the other student riders. It was what Indians call an "inauspicious" beginning that I tried not to read too much meaning into.

The first motorcycle dealer, a small solicitous man, wanted to sell to Thomas, being a man in a man's world, and turned his back on me when, after Thomas stomped away irritated by the man's misplaced persistence, I approached. He rolled his eyes dubiously at me then turned and disappeared through a shabby curtain at the back of the showroom. When he didn't return, I got the message: he didn't sell motorcycles to women.

Men may have designed motorcycles for their own adventures, but that never stopped women from riding. Americans Effie Hotchkiss and her mother, Avis, rode round-trip, coast-to-coast in the United States on a Harley with a sidecar in 1915. Bessie Stringfield refused to let her gender or race hamper her. As a young, Black wife and mother devastated by the deaths of her three children, she turned to riding motorcycles in 1928, saying, "I'd toss a penny over a map, and wherever it landed, I'd go." Fifty years later, stuntwoman Marcia Holly rode a Kawasaki-based streamliner to set a land-speed record of 229.361 mph, becoming the first woman to break into the Bonneville 200 MPH Club. I wasn't in their league, but I had my own white whale to chase.

The second dealership's salesman harbored no such scruples about selling motorcycles to women. A worldly Sikh with rings on five fingers, Sahib Singh smiled, bearing a neat row of tiny red-stained teeth and nodding his turbaned head. I knew what I wanted: a black 350cc Standard Bullet with upgrades poached from the 500cc Deluxe—its dual-drum disc brakes, larger fuel tank, and locking toolboxes. She (motorcycles are feminine) should be all black like the goddess Kali, so a paint job was necessary, since the 500cc parts were gray. The price for my new, customized Bullet with a year's warranty and accident insurance (a bonus, given India's manic traffic), totaled 25,000 rupees ($1,400 U.S.).

A week after placing my order, one of Singh's workers wheeled my Kali out to me and my heart thrummed. I was both awed and terrified by her power and beauty. Seeing her black body curved in a dancer's pose, her handlebars flared as if enraged, her headlamp a bold unblinking eye, I knew I'd given her the right name. She was a goddess.

काली

A few weeks after getting my Bullet, I arrived at Sheikh Sara Authority to take my driving license test. Some would debate the necessity of a foreigner getting a driver's license in India, but I wanted to be legal. As I climbed the dusty steps of the flat-faced government building, there wasn't a woman in sight—only men loitering under dusty neem trees, spitting streams of red *paan,* a mixture of betel leaf and areca nut that's widely chewed in India.

I'd picked up a driving manual a week earlier from a portly man named Mr. Dubashi in the Office of Inquiry. He'd gazed at me through owlish glasses, as if I were some curious species, when I'd ask for a manual. Upon my return, however, he greeted me enthusiastically, asking dramatically if I'd studied the contents. His childlike excitement didn't fit with his stern Stalin-like stature and demeanor.

I'd driven for twenty-five years, so I'd only skimmed the driving manual, thinking that getting a permit in India would be similar to how I did it in the United States. But I was wrong.

Instead of handing me a written test, Mr. Dubashi pulled himself up and lumbered around to the end of the desk. He cleared the papers and pointed a fat finger at one of the many road sign images printed on a poster trapped under a thick plate of glass covering his desk.

"What is this?" he said, jabbing at an arrow that appeared to be doing a backbend.

"Ninety-degree turn," I said.

Without looking up, he shook his enormous head and stabbed another image. "What is this?"

It had two arrows, one short and straight with a second one bending to the right. "No passing," I said.

He waggled his head exuberantly then thumped a third symbol. "What is this?"

There was no mistaking it. "Train crossing."

Mr. Dubashi raised his sad eyes and furrowed his massive brow in disappointment. "Now you have *failed,*" he said. "Why you did not study the book I gave you?"

Failed? How could that be? I knew the symbols. I knew the rules. I just didn't know what he wanted. I stared at him, wondering if he expected me to offer an incentive to be granted a license. It wouldn't happen. I'd never bribed an official in any country, even when it made things easier. Easy wasn't my way.

Mr. Dubashi picked up the driver's manual and read aloud the correct responses for the symbols: *Curve Up Ahead; No Overtaking; Unguarded Level Crossing Ahead.* When he finished, I understood. I didn't mistake the meanings, I just hadn't memorized them verbatim, and Mr. Dubashi was a stickler.

We were silent awhile and then, not knowing what else to do, I smiled and asked, "Now what?"

He tipped his chair back on two legs, as if giving the options serious consideration, before dropping the chair to the floor with a thud and exclaiming, "I will pass you anyway."

On my way home, I fell in behind a truck full of female field hands sitting in the back like chicks in a nest. They listlessly rocked and swayed, their *dupatas* pulled over their coarse black hair. Their ages varied, with the wrinkled old women sitting closer to the cab, the younger women sitting near the tailgate, and the little girls fitted in here and there. Their *salwar kameezes* and *saris* were dusty and dirty from farming, and their arms were banded in colorful bangles. Smudged into the parts of some of the women's hair was *sindoor*, a red powder signifying who was married. Their ears were pierced with heavy earrings and nostrils discs of gold.

At first they took no notice of me, a lone biker trailing behind, swerving to miss the potholes that their driver thoughtlessly plowed through. Then boredom overcame one woman and her eyes began to follow me closely. She showed only mild curiosity at first, until—despite my head-to-toe garb of helmet, denim jacket, and leather gloves disguising my identity—something about me seized her imagination and her gaze deepened. She sat a little straighter and leaned closer to the tailgate, putting her calloused and cracked hands on the gate's peeling paint to steady herself. She trained her eyes on me for a long time before nudging the woman next to her. Together they watched me, and I them, wondering what made us so different beyond our obvious aesthetics. A moment later the two began poking and prodding the others. As the women and girls in the truck turned to see what was so urgent, their solemn faces cracked open one-by-one, revealing big white teeth and toothless grins as it dawned on them that the rider was a woman.

3

Gurus and Goddesses

The Royal Enfield Bullet motorcycle began as a crude bicycle known as a "bone shaker" in the mid-1800s in Hunt End, England. The Townsend Cycle was a strange contraption with an iron cross-frame, unequal wooden wheels fortified with iron strips, and wooden triangle pedals. Its peculiarities, however, didn't stop it from becoming wildly desired. Bicycles brought freedom.

The cycle infatuation eventually set fire to a hunger for not only freedom but speed, giving birth to the motorcycle in 1899. The Townsend Cycle morphed through a series of transformations and sputtered onto the scene as the Royal Enfield motorcycle in 1901. Over the next half-century, it evolved from a 125cc two-stroke engine to 350cc and 500cc four-strokes. By the 1950s, the word Bullet was added to its name, but evolutionary engineering stalled as manufacturing shifted from England to India. Few changes occurred between the 1950s model and the one I bought new in 1997. It's not the most muscular motorcycle but no other matched its thumping soul, or its cantankerous nature. Since it's prone to breakdowns, I'd need to know how to fix it when things went wrong. I needed someone to teach me basic Bullet maintenance.

I'm mechanically inclined, something I inherited from my dad. As a girl, I crept into the garage to watch him tinker with the family Oldsmobile as he pondered the engine's problem, finding solutions to whatever troubles presented. When my interests continued as I grew, he taught me basic car repairs while my older brother never figured out how to pop a hood.

Thomas introduced me to his mechanic Nanna, who had a reputation as a "quiet genius" who didn't enter relationships lightly. I hung around the shop on Saturday mornings with the other ex-pat riders, working up the courage to ask for his help and fearing he'd say no. When I finally asked Nanna to teach me basic repairs, he gazed at me as if I'd requested he translate the *Bhagavad Gita* before agreeing, telling me to come the next day for my first lesson.

I arrived at Nanna's shop, a cinderblock structure crouched under a flyover and crammed with forgotten and forlorn motorcycles with missing wheels, rusted cylinder heads, and split seats. Weeds worked their way through the spokes of the deserted bikes that littered his courtyard, burrowing into carburetors and snaking up to choke the controls. In the weeks I'd been going to the shop, I'd often wondered where all the motorcycles came from and how long they'd lingered like this. They looked like lost causes to me. As we sat sipping chai before my lesson started, I asked about them.

"What about that one," I asked, I pointed to a relic leaning against the fence. "What's its story?"

"The Norton? It belongs to a friend of mine."

His tone suggested the rider just dropped it off for a tune-up but its dry-rot tires, filler spilling from the split seat before cascading onto a corroded cylinder head, rusted chrome pipes, and rodent-gnawed cable casings said otherwise. Nanna read my mind as I stared at the once beautiful but now desolate bike.

"Only fifteen years," he said.

"Fifteen!" I cried.

"Yes."

"It's been here for fifteen years? Where's the owner?"

"He had to leave India suddenly."

"He's not coming back."

"He will, and I will keep it for him until he returns."

"And if he never returns?"

He gazed at me, the henna in his gray hair sparkling like a cap of copper wiring, as the corners of his mouth shifted imperceptibly to imply I knew nothing about what people would do. Finally he said, "Are you ready to learn?"

Nanna summarized the things I needed to learn. Mostly routine maintenance: setting tappets and timing, changing the oil, cleaning the spark plug, adjusting the chain, checking fluids, tightening loose bolts—as well as minor emergency repairs: fixing broken clutch and brake cables, repairing ruptured fuel lines, and changing flat tires. He wanted me to know the overall workings of the Enfield too, so that if major repairs were needed I'd understand what a mechanic was doing, even if I didn't do the work myself.

"You will find boys with tools all over India thinking they can fix your Kali. They cannot," he said. "They do not know Bullets, but you will."

Over the next two weeks, Nanna scrutinized me wrenching bolts and threading cables through clips and rings. He explained how the crankshaft rotated the pistons down into the cylinder head, sucking a mixture of air and fuel into the carburetor. I jotted it all down in my notebook: blend, trapped gasses, pistons top-dead-center, plug ignites spark.

In truth, I understood little. Motorcycles weren't like cars. His explanation of the engine sounded like the song "Dem Bones" from my childhood: *Toe bone connected to the foot bone, foot bone connected to the heel bone*, and so on, that I didn't really grasp. Instead, I simply wrote it all down and hoped it made sense when I needed it.

One afternoon, flies buzzing at my ears and eyes in the sweltering heat as I scribbled some esoteric point he made, I wondered aloud if I really needed to comprehend all the minutia. Nanna stared at me in dismay, asking, "How is it you can decide what is important and what is not until you understand all of it?"

Nanna was a man of few words but when he spoke I often felt two things were being said. I wondered, were we talking about motorcycles or was he teaching me some sort of metaphor for life? Did he mean that more than a basic understanding was always required to determine one's future? Or did he simply want me to know how an internal combustion engine operated?

Nanna didn't wait for me to figure out his koan, instead he expertly loosened the screws on the cam cover with his blunt fingers and removed the plate before pointing to the gap in the breaker points, a mechanism that reminded me of the bobbin section of a sewing machine.

"This gap sets the engine's timing to make it run smooth. It is important you have the width just right, but you will not have the tool to do this."

I waited for him to continue, wondering why I wouldn't have these tools since the gap was so slight. Were they bulky? Were they expensive? Were they not available in India?

"There is no need to carry so many things," he continued. "India will provide for you." To prove his point, he glanced around until he located a discarded cigarette box in the dust at the gate of his shop, and told Poppy, one of his two young mechanics, who was lovingly styling his Bollywood-esque hair in a mirror, to bring it to him. "This," he said, tearing off the flap and holding it up for my inspection, "can measure both the timing and spark plug gaps accurately. Fold it once and you have a gauge for setting the timing, fold it two times to set the spark plug's gap width."

Why not just carry the little tool? I thought. How cumbersome could a set of gap measures be? But I didn't ask that, instead I squawked, "*Garbage?* You want me to use garbage to keep Kali running?"

Something settled onto Nanna's otherwise agreeable face, the weary expression of a savant saddled with an idiot. His disappointment pained me, and my mind scrambled to understand his meaning before it clicked. It wasn't about having a tool, but using the tool I already possessed—my mind—to solve any problems.

I recalled my dad teaching me to change air filters and sand carbon off spark plugs in our garage, the scent of a warm oily engine filling my nostrils. He would approve of Nanna's creed, although rubbish wouldn't be his choice of gadget either. The message, however, to be unburdened and resourceful in life was familiar. Years earlier, while hiking in Shawnee National Forest with a boyfriend, he took a photo of me sitting on a boulder that he later gave me as a gift. Under the image he'd inserted a quote from Juvenal—a late first-century AD Roman poet—that read, *Travel light and you can sing in the robber's face.*

Nanna pushed this philosophy further, insisting I not only do away with stuff but that I benefit from what others left behind. This ideology was foreign to me. I liked shiny new things and thought each item served just one purpose—as if it had only one life.

While learning to repair Kali, I had Nanna customize her, replacing her bench seat with a handmade single-saddle, and painting Kali in Hindi—काली—in gold on the sides of her tank. The lettering had two meanings, Kali—the goddess and bud—a small flower. My dad's nickname was Bud.

My years of hanging out in the garage watching my dad gave way to other interests as I became a teenager, and the two of us spent little time together. One day, when I was thirteen he uncharacteristically stopped me in the hall and proclaimed, "You can go anywhere. Do anything. Be anyone you want."

My dad, a man of few words and fewer hugs, was a breadwinner, not a nurturer. Nor were we a touchy-feely family prone to expressing our emotions. He fiercely loved his family in the best way men of the 1950s and 1960s were expected to, by giving us all the things he could afford to buy. But he knew I lacked conviction in myself, despite years of confidence-boosting activities—dance, swimming, horseback riding lessons—my parents gave me. It hurt his heart to see his little girl, his Little Lou Lou, Connie Luigi, Squeegee, Weegee—his nicknames for me, expressions of his quiet love—not grasp her potential, not believe in herself. It drove him to do what fathers of his era left to mothers: deliver encouraging words.

You can go anywhere. Do anything. Be anyone you want.

My teenage brain couldn't comprehend this. It reeled wildly at how wrong he was about me. The person he saw wasn't who I added up to be. I slithered along walls. I remained mute around others. I cringed from attention.

I stood dumbfound as his alien concepts of my capability echoed through me. The silence between us grew, turning a tender father-daughter moment awkward. Neither of us knew what to say or do next, so we crept past each other without another word. But, a kernel of his belief was seeded in me.

Years later, on January nine, my twenty-third birthday, one week after my dad turned fifty-three, he died suddenly of a heart attack.

After his death, I often wondered if he somehow knew he'd die young and never get to see me flourish. Knew he'd never live to see if I overcame my self-doubt. I'll never know, but his Can-Do faith began to slowly and quietly bloom in me, becoming my mantra. A tattoo imprinted on my soul. A belief that carried me through life, and the coming five months and nearly 7,000 miles as I rode on the edge of India.

4

The Hand of God

In 1992, five years before setting out on a Bullet solo around India, I was a proofreader for a pharmaceutical company when it announced its down-size and relocation from the Midwest to the East Coast. Prior to that, I'd spent nine years on the company's assembly lines inspecting pill bottles as they jostled by before taking an educational leave of absence to earn a degree in journalism (after switching my major from anthropology). I'd returned to the company with hopes of climbing the corporate ladder and had been in my job for two years when the downsizing was announced.

My colleagues and I feared our jobs would be eliminated in the move. The factory was staying put but many of the office positions were headed east. While my teammates dreaded the possibility of being relocated or becoming redundant, I viewed it as a chance to leave my hometown and live a larger life, one I'd been too scared to chase after earning my degree. I'd settled for safe instead, but in the time I'd been back, I'd felt as if I didn't belong, as if there was more for me elsewhere. This was my chance.

As we waited for our sealed envelopes containing our fates in the form of an offer or a pink slip, I envisioned my transformative new life in Princeton, New Jersey, a train ride away from the culture and sophistication of New York City. The day we received our notices, my coworker brought in photos of her recent trip to Germany. Sandy planned to retire early and welcomed the buyout package we'd be offered if our positions were eliminated or we declined the offers. She loved to travel abroad and often asked me where I'd like to go. I had no desire to go overseas and was content to climb into my car and head out, more for the thrill of driving and being in motion than the destination.

When my boss delivered the envelope containing my future, I was looking at Sandy's photos, images of her trip to Europe were spread across my desk. Pulling the offer from the envelope, I sucked in a sigh of relief as I read the opening line: "We are pleased…" before skimming the page in search of my new job title and salary. Disappointed, I saw "proofreader" and the salary I currently earned. The work wasn't fulfilling, but the money provided a good living in southern Indiana.

Accompanying the offer was a cost-of-living breakdown revealing I couldn't afford to live in Princeton and would have to commute from the deep suburbs. As the reality of what my future looked like dawned on me, my fantasy of living a high life in an intellectually rich city a short train ride from the City That Never Sleeps dissolved. In its place emerged a life in a cookie-cutter, thinly walled apartment in a mundane complex on the outskirts of everything while commuting to a dismal job of proofreading pharmaceutical package inserts all day as my mind numbed and spirit dulled.

It didn't take a genius to figure out I wouldn't be moving up but rather stagnating, or worse—sinking. I'd earned a degree in journalism from Indiana University's Ernie Pyle School of Journalism. I wanted to write stories not spellcheck documents no one read. I'd hoped the relocation offer would springboard me into a writing position with the company; a gateway to a new life. That possibility suddenly looked as unreachable as the far bank of the cold Ohio River white-capping outside my winter window.

Putting the depressing thoughts aside, I returned to Sandy's photos, hoping the pretty pictures would clear my gloom. The images weren't exceptional. No castles or century-old church spires pierced the sky, only traditional old German homes with red doors, thick thatched roofs, and flower boxes bulging with red and white geraniums. Yet, there was something beguiling about them. Until then, I told myself I was okay with a decent job, a good salary, a good life without questioning what "good" meant. Now, something inside me shifted as I examined first the photographs and then the slim sheet of paper predicting my future in black and white. One path offered security, income, and advancement, while the other promised.... What?

I went to sleep that night sure I'd soon be living on the East Coast commuting to a drab office—what else could I do—but woke the next morning with a new plan. Quit. Travel the world.

I'd never ranged far from home—one or two days' drive tops. Now the notion of exploring a wider world, walking among people whose languages and cultures shocked my Midwestern sensibilities, seemed the only path possible. It was as if the hand of God had pushed me forward. I'd never felt so simultaneously out of and in control of my life.

I took the buyout and gave up my apartment. I sold my car, suits and furniture, and bought a backpack and the cheapest one-way ticket to Europe—Frankfort, Germany—with a plan to be away at least six months but no more than twelve; any longer, I thought, might put me in danger of not coming back.

Friends threw me a going away party and presented me with useful gifts—electronic language translator, guide books, and cash —bundled into a bandana tied to the end of a long stick, signifying my new hobo status. When they asked "why," I couldn't tell them I felt trapped in an ordinary life in an ordinary job in an ordinary city, and longed for excitement and freedom. But more than that, I needed to prove something to myself. I couldn't say that aloud, couldn't risk hearing it, so I simply smiled and shrugged. In their eyes I read envy along with fear. A fear I refused to acknowledge, instinctively knowing if I did I'd never get away.

I left the United States in September of 1992 on an overnight Greyhound bus bound for Chicago's O'Hare International Airport and a series of flights destined for Germany. In my 40-gallon backpack, I'd stuffed a two-person tent, three-season sleeping bag, inflatable air mattress, camp stove, extra fuel cylinders, two small lanterns powered by candles along with six extra candles, three dry bags and a dozen freezer bags, three pairs of cargo pants that converted into shorts, eight T-shirts, ten pairs of underwear, four sport bras and two regular bras, five pairs of thick hiking socks, a pair of sandals, a pair of shower shoes, a travel-size blowdryer, water purification tablets, a collapsible shovel (to responsibly bury excrement), shampoo, conditioner, a small comb and brush, makeup and mascara remover (I'm not sure why), a Swiss Army Knife, sunglasses, glasses, two guidebooks—Rick Steve's *Europe Through the Back Door* and *Europe on $40 a Day*—and three or four novels, one of which was *Iberia* by James A. Michener, that I've still never read.

My mom, grandmother and a friend saw me off at the bus station. All day leading up to boarding the bus my stomach churned and my mouth felt cottony at the thought of what I'd set into motion. As I climbed the metal bus steps, unwilling to show my nervousness, my grandmother turned to my mom and asked, "Are you really going to let her go?" Mom, who'd always encouraged me to live life my way, wouldn't try to stop me as my grandmother would have done to her, even if she was scared for me. We all knew the time for putting on the brakes had passed.

Once on the bus my stomach settled and excitement grew, until I landed in Frankfort and disembarked the plane. For hours I sat in the cavernous international airport's lobby/train terminal paralyzed by the thought of what I'd gotten myself into. At my side was my too-heavy backpack, bulging with perceived essentials. Hugging my waist was a money belt stuffed with thousands of dollars in American Express Travelers Cheques, expected to last a year if I was frugal. I'd never exchanged money in my life, couldn't read the twenty-four-hour clock the European trains ran on—had never ridden a train.

Around me fluttered voices of travelers in languages I couldn't understand headed for their ultimate destinations. I had no real plan. My plan was to arrive, after that it was vague.

Night filtered in through the terminal's high windows and I knew I had to get up and go. Somewhere. Anywhere. Just go.

For the next two years I crisscrossed my way in and out of Germany, Switzerland, Austria, Italy, Greece, Egypt, Jordan, Syria, Turkey, and the Czech Republic. I often traveled in the company of others by bus, boat, train, and even donkey cart— but always at the mercy of someone else's timetable. Someone else's route. Ready for a change, I headed to India.

5

On the Road

I'd planned the journey for months, addressing every conceivable necessity for success, but when the alarm rang at 4:30 a.m., on the day of departure, I burrowed down under the sheet. I woke hours later, my head stuffy from the sun-heated room, and tried to convince myself it was too late to leave. Traffic would be heavy and slow-going, and I loathed New Delhi's crawling congestion. But I'd already postponed my start twice for little reasons, and friends were becoming doubtful I'd do it.

The "Ready, Set" part of any plan was easy for me, but I stalled when it came to "Go." From the corner of the room, I sensed my packed-and-ready-to-go saddlebags eyeing me judgmentally and knew Kali awaited two floors below. All I had to do was load up and leave, but I stayed in bed. Finally, I brokered a deal with myself: it did not matter how far I rode so long as I got on the road.

I shuffled barefoot into the kitchen and found Thomas and his wife Luise making coffee. I'd been staying with them in their Nizamuddin apartment since giving up mine two streets over. The espresso machine, a gleaming chrome Italian contraption I coveted, hissed milk into a luxurious froth as the rich aroma of Arabica beans suffused the sunny kitchen. Luise fixed me a farewell cappuccino and I leaned against the counter sipping it and surveying the airy apartment. I hadn't left yet and I already missed my friends and the safe feeling of belonging that comes with a place.

Luise's serious eyes studied me, and I hoped she wasn't wondering if I was really going this time. I'd overstayed my welcome and wore their generosity thin. I didn't blame them for wanting me out, I wanted me out too. I dithered, chit-chatting about how hot and dry it was until Thomas offered to carry some of my gear downstairs to Kali, and I retrieved my saddlebags and daypack.

I'd packed my bags carefully, loading my daypack with my journal, favorite pens, notes taken while working with Nanna, my Nikon camera, two lenses, and a compass. Items that spoke to an identity I'd created as a writer and storyteller. They gave me a sense of security and purpose that counterweighted the imposter lurking inside me. Writers were brave and fearless. They spoke the truth. I kept my truth hidden most of my life, projecting an image I hoped matched the fantasy in my head: an intrepid woman. Over the course of my life, I'd willed myself brave, bold, fearless whenever I encountered something in life that scared me. From the stuffed bear looming in a shadowy corner in the museum, to sitting alone watching spooky movies in the dark, to quitting a "good job" and boarding a Greyhound bus bound for Chicago to get on planes to Europe and eventually India.

I slung the saddlebags containing two T-shirts, five pairs of underwear, one sport bra, a couple pairs of socks, basic toiletries, shower shoes, guidebooks, and a few other miscellaneous items over my shoulder. It weighed nothing compared to the blue behemoth I'd carried when I boarded that Greyhound bus years earlier.

Downstairs, I lashed a five-gallon jug of oil to Kali's crash guards, since Bullets notoriously leaked. Flopping the canvas saddlebags over the rack I'd had Nanna fit on Kali, I tied it to the frame with old bootlaces and secured the tote with bungee cords, before unlocking the heavy padlock and chain I kept snaked around the front forks. Lastly, I wrapped a thin cotton *dupatta* around my face and neck, the scarf helped keep out the dust, and pulled on my jacket, gloves, helmet, and purple daypack. The gear hid my gender and created a barrier between me and everyone else. A woman on a motorcycle would draw a lot of unwanted attention. As a woman alone in the world, I got tired of being an obvious woman alone in the world. This way, people would assume I was male and a foreigner; no Indian dressed as I did, especially in temperatures that soared above 120 degrees Fahrenheit in the summer. The getup probably didn't channel badass, more likely Ninja Turtle with my purple pack and mismatched clothes. Underneath it all, however, I felt fierce.

The neighborhood—a colony clustered with large white homes butted against a brick wall surrounding Humayun's Tomb, a 16th-century emperor—stirred. A pair of gardeners in the park across from Thomas and Luise's home clipped the grass with long thin scissors, as a *subzi* wallah pushed his lopsided cart down the street hawking vegetables and calling, "*Tamatar. Aloo. Pyaj.*" I took in the familiar surroundings one last time, missing New Delhi already even though I sometimes hated it, and climbed onto Kali, kickstarting her to life. As they waved goodbye, Thomas grinning enviously and Luise smiling warmly, I suppressed my nervousness and rolled on the throttle.

I'd washed and waxed Kali the day before, greasing her saddle with so much silicon that it made staying on her difficult as I slipped through the city's colonies. I rolled past Safdarjang's bustling market, its rippling scent of overripe guavas and bananas bidding me goodbye, then Lodi Garden where a few old men strolled among the jasmine grounds in crisp white kurtas, before reaching Chanakyapuri where foreign consulates sat imperiously on lush lawns. On the outskirts of town, beyond the sculpted and spotless diplomatic area, were shanties. There, squat buildings squeezed together were awash with hand-painted signs advertising hair tonics and spicy snacks in vivid, garish colors. Thick, black, electrical lines sprouted from poles like cobras from a basket, coiling into the sky before snaking illegally into shops and homes.

I got turned around in that part of town and tried to sidle up to a rickshaw to ask the driver directions to National Highway 8 but failed to stop Kali and bumped into it, sliding out of the saddle and onto the tank. The passenger, a policeman, peered out at me unhappily as I steadied myself; his irritated expression quelled my request for directions.

I eventually found my way and ramped onto National Highway 8 headed for Pushkar, in Rajasthan, famous for its camel fair and the location of the first shakti peetha temple on my list. The sun sizzled my back and New Delhi's smelly urban settlements gave way to green fields and the sharp fresh scent of tilled earth covered in bright-yellow mustard farms. Men with coconut-oiled hair no longer hustled along city sidewalks toting briefcases, instead women labored under bundles of scythed grass, ancient sickles swinging at their sides. I goosed Kali's throttle, picking up speed, the rushing air cooling the sweat slicking my body under my heavy, head-to-toe gear. Comforted by Kali's purr and to finally be on my way, I relaxed.

I settled into a steady pace of fifty mph—a tune popping into my head about a bullfrog named Jeremiah (where it would loop for the rest of the journey)—before coming to a halt just outside Gurgaon. In the stalled traffic, I was trapped in a line of overheated, circus colored Tata trucks, their diesel engines snorting like beasts. Dozens of third eyes—the spiritual gateway to higher consciousness—stared at me from the trucks' bumpers. Alongside each eye was the ubiquitous command, "Horn Please," the Golden Rule for navigating India's traffic.

The exhaust fumes from the vehicles curled around me, intensifying my impatience, and I crept Kali between two trucks to see what the holdup was. The road shimmered with vibrating trucks, buses, and cars but offered no reason for the gridlock or expectation of movement. Feeling anxious and trapped, I fought the urge to shed my gear. My body swelled in the heat now that I'd stopped, and the red and green dupatta felt like a noose around my neck.

Life along the edge of the bottleneck moved freely. A boy rolled a bicycle rim along the shoulder, guiding it with a stick while his friends ran after him laughing as their bare feet, hardened from a lifetime of shoelessness, pounded the solid earth. On the sidewalk, a cluster of Sikhs swathed in plum, saffron, and teal turbans discussed business or politics near a paan wallah, the *Financial Times* and *Times of India* tucked under their hairless arms. Women burdened with shopping bags burbled around them. A mongrel dog picked at blackened pieces of fruit a wizened sweeper rucked into a garbage pile.

A boy in shorts and a saggy undershirt wove his way between the rumbling trucks, scanning for customers to sell his marigold garlands. The blood-orange offerings for the gods ensured safe passage. Most of the truckers around me displayed them from rearview mirrors. I considered buying one too, but I didn't like to think of myself as superstitious and not in control of my destiny —even though I read my horoscope daily and once had my fortune told by a parrot on a beach in Goa. The bird, working at its owner's behest, forecast my future by selecting a card from an array of ordinary playing cards before proffering a raspy chirp and hopping back into its cage. Its owner's interpretation of its prognostication was equally incomprehensible. But that was just for fun. I didn't take such prophecies seriously, any more than I did the prediction of the woman I'd shared a cabin with while studying Hindi in the Himalayan foothills.

Maureen had come to India to study astrology and wanted to practice her skills on me. I didn't like her; she was accusatory and walked around the three-room cabin farting—things I didn't know before agreeing to share it with her for a month. One chilly evening as I stoked the fire in the potbellied stove, I relented to her harassment to forecast my future and told her my birth vitals. She keyed the date and time I was born into her laptop's special software program—her high-tech crystal ball. When my astrological birth chart appeared on her screen, revealing a blueprint to my past and future. She scowled. My moon would soon afflict one of my rising houses, she said; or maybe it was my sun would soon conjunct with one of my signs. It sounded like gobbledygook, and my expression (I don't have a poker face) broadcast my cynicism. Maureen enjoyed being the bearer of bad news and gleefully clarified the chart's meaning, "If you ride your motorcycle between May and October, you'll either be severely injured or killed."

I thought Maureen's prediction was hogwash. She knew that was the timeframe I'd be riding, and wanted to scare me since she didn't like me anymore than I did her. Besides, I was a Capricorn, a pragmatic goat and nonbeliever in superstitions. I favored physical protection and dressed in substantial gear designed to minimize injuries in case of a crash.

My overdressed state and large black helmet caused the boy selling leis to shy around me like a spooked horse, veering past with wide eyes. As he did, I looked into the cab of the diesel rumbling next to me. Its driver had invested heavily in the gods' protection. A plump rope of papaya-orange florets swayed from the rearview mirror of the tricked-out truck. A fringe of gold tinsel dripped from his windshield and incense smoldered on the dash before the images of Krishna—the blue god who symbolized love and destroyed sin, Hanuman—the monkey god who represented strength and perseverance, and Ganesh—the elephant-headed god and lord of beginnings who eliminated obstacles. The trucker's precautions made me wonder if I should reconsider my resistance to the leis, but the boy had disappeared into the thicket of trucks and buses.

The traffic still wasn't moving, so I shifted Kali into neutral and reached down into my saddlebag to confirm my maps and list of shakti peetha temples were securely stowed. I had an irrational concern I'd lose them and consequently be unable to find my way to the temples. I carried three English-language, German-made maps Thomas and Luise gave me. Each map covered a section of India's west, south and east, as well as a Hindi Indian-made atlas. I used the two in tandem. The meticulously illustrated German maps were fastidiously accurate, denoting every road, mountain range, river, and desert in artistic details of earthy sage and smoky grays. Thick red veins announced major highways and pink dashes suggested lesser-traveled roads. As beautifully designed as they were, they failed in one aspect: they were written in English. I needed the Hindi maps to know how to pronounce the town and village names, if I hoped to find the shakti peetha temples.

The traffic splintered after fifteen minutes and I was soon clocking Kali at fifty mph down National Highway 8. Angling southwest through Gurgaon into Haryana, I headed into Rajasthan, dodging oncoming drivers as they drifted drunkenly across lanes. Their unwanted games of chicken forced me onto the shoulder, increasing my agitation and ratcheting the muscles in my neck and shoulders as a string of curses spewed out of me. Distracted by my efforts to stay alive, I didn't notice a moody bank of clouds marching toward me.

6

Angry Gods

Tucked into the far western corner of the sky was a churning mass of angry energy that blotted the light from all around and spun out muscular winds like an advancing war party. July is monsoon season in western India, when storms drench the parched land with rains of such force that thousands die in drownings, landslides, or electrocutions. In cities, children and adults fall into open uncovered sewers, the manhole lids stolen and sold for the metal, and are swept away. I understood the danger the season brought to cities, but didn't think it would be a problem in the rainless Thar Desert, the direction I was headed: counterclockwise around India, an inauspicious direction I later learned.

Within seconds, the black clouds stretched from horizon to heaven, threatening to release a torrent of rain. I recalled a place a few miles back that offered protection, but I had a rule in life: no backtracking. Hoping to outrun the storm, I twisted Kali's throttle until the speedometer needle quivered at sixty mph. The throbbing thunderheads swiftly smothered the land in shadow, as the winds bullied Kali and me around. Grains of sand pecked my neck, chest, and wrists. I tensed. Focusing on the road, I gripped Kali tight as a snarky voice reminded me of Maureen's prophecy.

No one—including me—knew the exact route I was taking, nor precisely how long I'd be gone. There was no way for anyone to get in touch with me, nor did I have contacts on the road: no friends or friends of friends to offer help. No one expected me to call daily or even weekly. I called when I found a phone, when I found the time, or when I made the time. The closest thing I had to a tether was calling my mother the first of each month, but even that had grace periods. I'd purposefully designed my journey so I'd be free and disconnected. Sensing the cost that came with that choice, I now wondered if I'd regret it.

The wind whipped up the sand and it nipped at my exposed flesh. The heavens yawned, releasing fat drops that pelted me like buckshot, distorting my vision through the helmet's visor and bleeding the colorless world around me into a dark smear. Thunder drowned out Kali's roar as I accelerated to sixty-five, sixty-eight, seventy miles an hour, causing her to shudder. The rain hammered me. My heart raced. Some cars and trucks pulled to the side of the road, but others kept moving. It seemed safer to keep riding and find shelter rather than make myself a target by sitting on the side of the road while the gods' bellowed *Go home, girlie.*

As crosswinds rammed me, I glimpsed the yellow eyes of oncoming cars and braced myself to be swamped by their splashing water. "Keep calm," I cautioned myself, fearful of hydroplaning as the road streaked beneath me in a vicious yowl. A voice inside me warned, *Slow down. You're going too fast.* I backed off the throttle, dropping to forty, then thirty.

I was searching for a roadside cafe or other business to escape into when I saw a billboard announcing a *haveli* up ahead.

As I approached the turn to the cafe, I realized the road disappeared under water. Unsure of the road's condition beneath the swirling surface, and not wanting to risk a punctured tire or bent rim, I continued on the highway. It dipped and swelled like the ocean. At the top of each crest I hoped I'd see a refuge, but each time saw nothing but more empty grayness.

Finally, a gas station appeared in the distance. I uttered a prayer that the pumps had canopies over them, but they stood naked. The office several yards away offered a lip jutting from its façade and I squeezed Kali under it, shutting the engine off and letting my nerves dial down. The rain plunged over the roof and pounded the hard earth, barely chiseling a trench in it. Depleted, I sat in the water-filled saddle, unable to move and thanked the goddesses for keeping me alive, unaware I was being watched.

7

Through the Looking Glass

Shivering, I heeled down the kickstand and eased Kali onto her side. I needed to get warm and dry, but there was no easy way to dismount. Although I didn't carry much luggage, I'd piled it high and topped it off with my sleeping bag, making swinging my leg over the saddle cumbersome when dry and impossible when wet. My only option was to slide off, hauling my right leg across the saddle like a carcass. My body groaned as I unfolded it from an S-shape. Standing, fatigue consumed me and I steadied myself before peeling off my gear. My water-logged leather gloves sucked at my skin like leeches. When I finally tugged my hands free, I saw the cheap leather had stained my skin black.

The building's lip didn't provide enough cover to keep my things dry, so I rummaged around in my saddlebag for my poncho to wrap around my sleeping bag. I'd learned long ago that beds in the kind of hotels I stayed in didn't always have clean sheets, and if I was going to sleep in something dirty it should be my own grime. As I tucked the poncho around the sleeping bag, I noticed the three men inside the service station. A burly mustachioed man with hair that resembled a curled-up cat sat behind a desk with a newspaper spread before him, and two whippet-thin, barefooted men with rolled-up trousers fought the water spilling into the office with long-handled squeegees. The manager's eyes didn't budge from the paper, but the other two drank me in, contorting their necks to look at me without the boss noticing.

Even though the office offered warmth and protection, I didn't want to call more attention to myself by walking through the front door. Instead, I stepped into a phone booth attached to the end of the building, closed the door, and leaned my head against the cloudy glass. My wet clothes constricted my movements, making it difficult to breathe. Everything about me was heavy, tight, and soaked. Even my boots were filled with water.

The thirsty earth couldn't absorb the rain and it puddled outside the booth. Within minutes the floor flooded, forcing me to step up on a small ledge. As the rains continued to come down, the water in the booth rose. Staying in it meant staying wet. The only alternative was inside the office with the men.

A sliding glass window separated the booth and office. I'd kept my back to the men and now turned to see if anyone watched me. As a woman alone in the world, I was used to the stares of men—some curious, some predatory, all uncomfortable. Being tall, blond, and unaccompanied by a man made me fair game for their unwanted hands and crude propositions. In a nation with half a billion males, putting up with stares was a constant, and I longed for invisibility. Since cutting my long hair into a pixie for this journey I'd become less interesting. Long hair made me womanly in India; short hair was what widows, valueless to society, wore. I didn't like the idea of walking through the front door, of putting myself in their spotlight, and crazily wondered if I could crawl through the window without being noticed.

The boss thumbed the pages of his *Hindustan Times*, working a wad of *paan* in his jowl, while the workers continued their watery crusade. I eased the window halfway open, testing to see if anyone would look. The office lights were out, casting it in twilight as a percussion of rain drummed the flat roof. I pushed the window fully open and waited. The men didn't acknowledge this, emboldening me. Leaning in, I placed my helmet and gloves onto one of three chairs inside. As I did, one of the workers heard me and turned. We eyeballed each other and I held my breath. His partner sensed he was working alone and turned toward me. The three of us gaped at each other, their expressions curious and mine a grimace. I waited for them to make a fuss. They didn't. Instead, they turned away and resumed sluicing out the water, while the boss remained engrossed in the national news.

Committed to keep going, I hoisted my leg all the way through the window. Half in and half out, I tapped my foot around, searching for solid ground. Finding it, I began tugging the rest of my body into the office. I thought I'd made it until my jacket snagged on the latch. Pinned in place, I flailed like a fish on a hook. The window clattered and refused to let go as I dangled stupidly on the sill, struggling to free myself. I finally did and spilled inside onto a chair. No one turned to look or paid the slightest attention as I stripped off my jacket and leaned back in the chair. Teeth chattering and dripping puddles on the floor the men would mop up later, I closed my eyes and let sleep take over.

I woke, my clothes still damp, to sunny skies, unsure how long I'd napped. The sweepers were gone but the man behind the desk continued to read his paper as if nothing had occurred. But something had: I'd survived my first test. I was still standing. Still in one piece. Gathering my stuff, I strolled out the door, my boots hammering the floor as I headed for Kali. Only then did I feel the boss' eyes on me.

काली

The highway smoked like lava as I opened the throttle wide to let the speed dry my clothes. A few miles down the road the land was bone dry. Tumbleweeds lingered along the highway, waiting for a brisk breeze to set them rolling, the reek of dung and decay returned to the air, and vultures circled overhead. The road spilled out ahead of me in a long, thin black line before disappearing into the horizon.

It took an hour to reach Jaipur and another to find the hotel I'd preselected from my guidebook. It offered a *chowkidar* to guard Kali. Indian men couldn't keep their hands off Bullets. I'd caught several of them straddling Kali in New Delhi, pretending to ride her while twisting her knobs and switches. If I could have, I'd have rolled her into the hotel room with me, as everything else came inside: saddlebags, canvas tote, sleeping bag, backpack, and oil jug that I strapped to the crash bars.

The hotel's lobby was a small but light-filled space with faded hummingbird-blue walls and a crimson tribal banner draped over a teak check-in counter. I crossed the marble floor, leaving a fine trace of sand in my wake, while outside Kali listed on her stand. The clerk inclined his head and smoothed the wide lapels of his maroon blazer as I asked for a single room with a desert cooler.

"Sorry, madam. No single rooms, only double," he said. "Very nice double room."

I was tired and suspicious of his motive, thinking he was conning me into a costlier room; I'd traveled around long enough to know when I was being gamed. I was about to accuse him of this when he added, "It is the same price as a single for you, madam."

Feeling inadequate, I thanked him and signed the register. Behind me two young bellhops tussled to see who'd fetch my bags and earn a tip. The bigger boy won by smacking the little one on the head and he followed me out to Kali. A bag in each of his hands, he led me to a capacious room with an attached bathroom. My New Delhi apartment had been equipped with Western amenities: a shower with hot and cold running water and a sitting toilet with a seat. I wouldn't find these luxuries in the budget hotels I stayed in; they'd have squat toilets with single open faucets, and buckets with plastic cups hanging on the side for bathing.

I filled the bucket with water from a tank stored on the roof and added washing powder I'd dug from my bag, then stripped off my T-shirt, sport bra, panties, socks, and wrapped a *lungi*, a thin blue and pink sheet of cotton I strolled beaches in, around myself. Stuffing the clothes into the sudsy bucket, I vigorously agitated the bundle until my arms tired, then rinsed and strung everything about the room to dry before running a fresh bucket for my bath.

The water was too hot to bathe with so I turned to the sink to wash my face. In the dim light and pitted mirror I saw a woman with wild hair and fierce eyes staring back. She was foreign yet familiar. That morning, I'd been reluctant to leave New Delhi, nervous about the unknown. That seemed a long time ago now. The road, the storm, the escape had peeled some part of me away, and I glimpsed a new me emerging.

8

Lost

I rose late and ate a leisurely breakfast at a cafe, lingering to write yesterday's adventure in my journal and a few letters to family and friends. The fat sun was hot and high in the sky by the time I finished poking around in the market square, treating myself to a silver necklace before heading back to the hotel to pack. Plucking the clothes I'd strewn around the room the night before, I rolled them into tight bundles and stuffed them into my saddle bags. Since I'd had trouble finding the hotel the night before, riding up and down roads for nearly an hour before locating it, I asked the desk clerk for directions out of town. A local could easily follow his left and right directions, noting landmark buildings I didn't know and likely couldn't find, but pressing him for more wasn't likely to improve the results.

It took almost as long getting out of town as it had getting in —all roads seemed to lead to the market square. Finally, I hit the one that took me to the highway. Clouds laced over the hot sun, and I grew anxious it would rain again. When light specks dotted my visor, I pulled under a burly old tree on the side of the road to wait it out. Across the road a leathery old man, crouched like a gargoyle and smoking a beedi, eyed me inscrutably. Two teen boys on a scooter wanted to join me under the tree, but I shook my head and they parked under another nearby, joining the old man in staring. When the rain didn't increase or let up, I shed my helmet, jacket, and gloves. The teens' twittered when I revealed myself, but the old man remained stoic. I imagined his X-ray vision saw through me with or without my getup. I imagined he thought all kinds of unkind things about me for being out there on my own—as respectable women didn't travel alone—but when the rain cleared and I readied to leave, he stood and saluted me.

The landscape grew hillier as I neared Pushkar—the Aravalli Range laying rumpled like a child's blanket. Smog drifted into the crevices of the ancient ridges and vultures wheeled in the gauzy sky like drifting flakes of ash. I reached back to check on my daypack. I no longer wore it strapped to my back because it was too heavy and had attached it to Kali's rack. But the rough roads loosen the straps and the pack kept slipping off, forcing me to keep checking it. This time, I discovered it hung precariously low and near the chain guard, so I pulled over to readjust it. Too hot and tired to get off Kali and secure it properly, I twisted around and half-heartedly re-cinched it, figuring it would be fine for a few miles. Pushkar and the day's end awaited just over the hill.

The mountain range between Ajmer and Pushkar is called Nag Pahar (Snake Mountain), and it offers a series of twists and turns that provided a relief to the monotonous hours of riding on straight flat roads. Kali purred through the curves as I leaned her into them, the rhythmic whooshes putting me in the zone of being "one with the bike" as my motorcycle instructors back home had insisted. I concentrated on the road and considered the surprises around the bends as I'd been taught, forgetting about everything but the road as the desert's soft beauty cleared my mind.

Arriving in Pushkar, I pulled into a tourist bungalow's parking lot and killed the engine, pausing for a moment to relish the day's fading glow as Kali's ticking engine slowed. Thankful my second day on the road wasn't as harrowing as the first, I swung my leg off Kali. It cleared the luggage easily. Too easily. Something was wrong. The bag was missing. A little voice chirped, *I told you so.*

Darkness falls fast in hill country and, if I hoped to find my bag, I needed to retrace my path quickly. The expensive camera and lenses inside would likely end up on the Black Market if someone found it first. Riding back the way I'd come, I scanned the road hoping to spot it whispering, "Please God. Please God" to no avail. All I saw were tumbleweeds and trash.

Halfway over the hill toward Ajmer, I heard the zuzz of a scooter and spotted a mountainous police officer on a little baby-blue Bajaj finning toward me. I stopped and waved my arms for help. He pulled over and stepped easily from the scooter and swaggered toward me. He had a face like a hangman's, dour and impassive, with a weighty handlebar mustache anchored by a big nose. As I tugged off my helmet and scarf, he delightedly exclaimed, "Madam!"

I launched into my troubles, my words ricocheting as uncertainty flickered across his face. He didn't get it. He couldn't grasp the importance of my stuff. Until that moment, I hadn't understood it either. Hadn't understood how much significance I'd attached to the items and the role they played in my life. The items in the bag were my connection to the me I knew. They defined my identity, centering me in my place in the world. With it all gone, I felt unmoored.

When he did not grasp my urgency, I heard myself lie. A lie I hoped would galvanize him into action.

"Heart," I said, thumping my chest. "Heart trouble. My medicine is in my missing bag," I pleaded while pantomiming what I hoped resembled reaching into a bag. Tears scored my cheeks and my body shook as waves of emotions swamped me: doubt, uncertainty, loneliness, apprehension, self-recrimination, insecurity, confusion, heartache, powerlessness, desolation, grief, vulnerability, loss, isolation, sorrow. It was too hard. All of it. The heat. The traffic. The storm. The dangerous drivers. Too impossible. Who was I to be out there? Why did I think I could do this? Why did I want to do this?

It was day two of my journey and I was only ninety-six miles from New Delhi. The gods knew I wasn't capable. They'd warned me. They'd thrown gauntlets in my path. They'd hurled rain as fat as fists at me. Now they'd grown weary of my slow wittedness and snatched the things that I clung to for legitimacy.

The officer's face darkened, contorting into worry as his brow crinkled. He scanned the surroundings, searching for someone to rescue him from this mad woman and make it right for both of us. When no one appeared, he resorted to the one thing he could do. He thrust his sequoia-like arms toward heaven and ordered me to "Be strong."

Cold water could not have been more effective.

Once I had myself under control, he launched into investigative mode, stopping the few cars, scooters, and pedestrians that came along. Everyone shook their head, and I imagined them saying, "*Nahin, nahin. Hum nay kuchnahin dekha hai,*" No, no, I have not seen a purple bag. Later, I learned he'd not been asking about my bag, but rather if they spoke English.

Three teenage boys packed onto one scooter spoke perfect Queen's English. Fashionably dressed in designer jeans and crisply pressed T-shirts, the boys translated for the police officer.

"Sorry, madam," said the first boy, shaking his head after I explained the situation. "You will never get your things back. Too many thieves in this area. There is always trouble here. I am sorry, but it is gone forever."

The officer swiveled and cocked his head like a mechanical bull between the boy and me, as the boy translated my trouble.

"You must go with the officer to Pushkar and file an F.I.R.," said the second teenager. "That is the proper thing to do."

"What's an F.I.R?" I asked.

"First Incident Report," said the third boy, not to be excluded.

"Will it help get my things back?"

"No," said the first teen, bobbling his head. "It is simply a formality. Your things are gone forever. You must accept this."

9

Waiting for a Sign

C aptain Dutt leaned forward in his chair at the police
station and asked, "Are you sure you were not robbed?"
The Captain and I faced each other over his sprawling desk.
The officer who brought me to the station was replaced by a
younger man who stood stiff outside the door awaiting the
Captain's orders. I wished I could tell him the bag was stolen
rather than admit my negligence; I might stand a better chance of
getting my things back if he thought they'd been stolen. But I'd
lied once, and it hadn't help.

I shook my head no and Captain Dutt extracted three sheets
of blank paper and two pieces of carbon paper from a desk
drawer. Layering them like a sandwich, he formed a packet and
secured the top with two straight pins. He looked bored now that
the notion of larceny was dismissed.

"Madam, please write your account of the incident and list all
the items in the bag," he said, handing me the papers and a pen.

As I scribbled, the young officer delivered a tea service. Not
chai, but English tea in dainty cups with silver vessels holding
thick cream and sugar cubes. Seeing the tea tray renewed my hope
that I might be important enough for a platoon of police to be

launched in search of my things. Chai was for ordinary occasions but English tea signaled a level of importance.

The officer settled Captain Dutt's cup and saucer in front of him and filled it with dark Darjeeling before plucking three cubes of sugar and a long dribble of cream that blushed it toffy. I finished the report and slid it across the desk to the captain, who read it while I fixed up my own cup of tea that the officer had left just out of my reach. As I sipped it halfheartedly, Captain Dutt called the young officer back into the room and ordered him to transcribe my statement into Hindi for the official report, or so I guessed.

"Madam, will you be staying in Pushkar long?" Captain Dutt asked once the officer retreated.

"When will I get my things back?" I knew my directness was rude, but my patience was gone. I no longer cared what impression I made.

"Madam, these matters take time," he said, lifting the rose-patterned teacup to his pursed lips, blowing and taking a long sip.

I left the police station and returned to the tourist bungalow under a starless, moonless night. The day's heat still hung in the air as I climbed the steps sprinkled with hundreds of ruby, Kali-tongue-like petals from an ancient bougainvillea that arched the hotel's entrance. Inside, I stood at the counter waiting for the dozing clerk to sense my presence so I could check in. He woke when I sniffed, and silently pushed a registration book the size of one of the stone tablets containing the Ten Commandments toward me as I handed him my passport. He had sympathetic eyes that I couldn't meet again as I signed and paid for two nights, hoping that gave the police enough time to recover my things.

"Second floor, madam," the clerk said. "Room end of hall."

I bent to pick up my bags and briefly met the clerk's kind eyes.

"Everything okay, madam?"

I nodded, unable to tell the story again and sure that by morning he'd have heard it anyway through India's incredible human-telecom system.

I didn't turn on the room's lights, instead fumbled my way around by moonlight filtering through the window. I sat numbly on the bed yearning to process my feelings in my journal as a means of fending off the doubt my mind conjured up about my fortitude, my judgment. Was the journey a mistake? If so many events happened in the first thirty-six hours, what other catastrophes awaited?

The room smelled of unwashed bodies as I stretched out on the bed, not bothering to unfurl my sleeping bag. The mattress was hard with a distinct dip in the middle from the weight of many others. I lay staring up at the ceiling, longing to sleep and wake to discover it had been a bad dream. But my mind whirled, refusing to shut off and casting self doubt. Outside the window the sky was as dark and empty as me. I knew there were only two choices: quit and return to New Delhi or keep going—with or without my things.

Alone in the dark, my mind feral with uncertainty, I longed to process the events and my feelings in my long-gone journal. Unable to do that, I tried to relinquish myself to some higher power, and prayed for a falling star or the piercing cry of a peacock, anything I could latch onto as a sign. But none came. The world remained eerily silent. I was on my own.

10

Wrists

Something happened during the night, and I woke the next morning resolved to give the police three days to recover my stuff. If they didn't, I'd leave regardless. In the meantime, Pushkar's Savitri temple, my first shakti peetha, held one piece of the goddess I'd come to collect.

I asked a hotel clerk for directions to the temple and he pointed to a shady path that ambled along the back of the hotel. It was the same man who'd checked me in the night before, and I wondered if I detected a note of sympathy in him as I headed into the heat with a bottle of water tucked under my arm.

The trail wove through a thatch of huts hemmed in by a stand of majestic magnolia trees, their dark waxy leaves holding back the sun like thousands of hands. I should have found the stroll charming and been grateful for the cool respite, but I moped along while scrawny dogs woofed at me and squealing children skittered after each other. Mothers squatting in doorways smiled at me as they braided snowy jasmine sprigs into their daughters' lush hair, while men, resembling rumpled sacks of laundry, lounged on charpoys, rope beds, smoking and regarding me with suspicion.

The shade abruptly ended several hundred yards from the base of the stairs leading to the temple. Giant slabs chiseled into the Aravalli Range offered a steep ascent. I wheezed, plopping down on one of the slabs every ten steps or so. My water bottle sweated as much as I did, as the cool water quickly warmed in the mid-morning heat. I trudged toward the top for half an hour before reaching the temple hovering serenely over the valley. Slipping out of my sandals, I stepped into the sacred space onto a cool marble floor that blessed my sweaty feet. Wide arches punctuated sky-blue walls, allowing a brisk breeze to billow my blouse as I went in search of the priest to ask what piece of the goddess the temple laid claim to.

In an altar room, I found two young European men whispering with their heads bent close. I moved away, not wanting to disturb them and not wanting to be disturbed by them. I expected the temple's priest to be a man but found a hawkish-nosed teenager wedged into a doorframe reading *The Hobbit*. He appeared too young to be a *pandit*, but the thread, a sutra, across his slight chest signaled his priestly Brahman status.

I greeted him, asking if he was the temple priest.

"My father is, but he cannot climb the mountain any longer, so I take his place. I'm Kamal," he said. "This temple has been in my family's care for hundreds of years."

Kamal lived alone in the temple, venturing to town weekly for food and water that he carried back up like a pack mule. I barely made the trip with one bottle of water and couldn't imagine doing it with much more.

Our chit-chat disturbed the Europeans, so Kamal rose, the hem of his creamy lungi spilling to the floor like milk, and motioned me to follow him as he weightlessly led the way. He led me to a room that hinted of burnt milk where a white terrier scuttled from under a *charpoy* snarling and showing its serrated teeth. I hesitated as Kamal swept a sinewy arm toward one of two chairs as he folded his limbs into the other like an idle marionette.

"The dog...," I said, nodding at the quaking creature glaring at me. It reminded me of my childhood dog, Bobbie. She was what my mom called a "Heinz 57," part Cocker Spaniel, part Border Collie, and part who-knows-what. Her personality had been distorted by cats that terrorized her as a puppy. Kamal's dog wasn't as adorable as Bobbie, but it had her dicey spirit. He plucked a shoe from a pile of sandals and lobbed it at the dog, causing it to reluctantly retreat under the charpoy. The mountain of shoes intrigued me, and I wondered why a barefoot priest owned them.

Under the charpoy, the dog transformed itself into something fiercer and edged its black nose into the open, emitting a low growl near my bare feet. I lifted them onto the chair.

"Is this a shakti peetha temple?" I asked, adding before he could respond, "Which piece of the goddess is here?"

My capacity for interaction with others, while naturally limited, had completely deserted me in the wake of my missing items. All I wanted was to learn which part of the goddess was in the temple so I could quickly withdraw to the solitude of my hotel room.

Kamal gazed at me over his protruding nose, perhaps pondering both my rudeness and question before saying, "Yes. The *manibandh*." He spoke dozens of languages he had picked up from tourists—English, French, German, Spanish, Japanese—but he didn't know the English word for the piece of the goddess. Instead, he pointed to his own delicate bones between his hand and forearm, tracing the bracelet of finely etched lines in the folds of his skin, to indicate "wrist." I looked at my wrists' lines, wondering what they meant. I'd later learn they indicated life expectancy, wealth, and fame in palmistry. Lines the gods gave each of us at birth to illustrate our destinies.

I waited for a sense of satisfaction at discovering my first piece of the goddess to settle in. For this success to banish my despondency over lost things. But nothing changed. I didn't feel magically empowered. I didn't feel anything.

The dog took the silence as a cue and crept out growling, twitching its black, button nose feverishly. Kamal lobbed another shoe and it scuttled back into its lair. I envied the dog's hidey-hole and stood to retreat to my hotel room.

11

Dumb Idea

"**M**adam must be placing ad in newspaper Lost and Found," the waiter said in English, surpassing my Hindi, as he refilled my coffee cup the next morning.

I listened out of fatigue rather than interest to his assertions, as I pushed my fried eggs around the plate. It had been two days since losing my bag, and the prospect of my things being returned seemed nil.

"Placing ad in paper is most effective," the waiter continued. "Your things come back to you. Everyone be reading ads."

The idea sounded ludicrous, given sixty percent of the nation's people could not read, but the waiter's persistence and sincerity prompted me to reconsider, and I asked him for directions to the newspaper office in Ajmer.

"Everyone be knowing. Ask anyone on street. They be helping you."

It seemed like a long shot but I had nothing to lose, and rode Kali to Ajmer. Once in town, I asked several people for directions to the newspaper and found that not "everyone" knew; everyone claimed to know but few gave the same directions. Indian hospitality dictates helping wayfaring strangers, but it didn't require giving the right help—something I discovered shortly after arriving in India, forcing me to adopt a best-two-out-of-three rule.

When I finally found the newspaper's office, the lights were out but several women floated about the room, the loose *pallus* of their saris riffling in their slipstreams. They paid no attention to me as I hovered in the doorway disheveled with helmet-sculpted hair, and neither did the men. They were hunched over heavy typewriters, dressed in matching tan safari suits and pounding out news from deep inside towers of stacked folders. I shifted on my feet and waited for someone to notice me. A man rushed past and paused long enough to ask what I wanted, *"Kya hai?"* and I told him. He rattled off what sounded like either a thousand or ten thousand rupees as the cost of an ad. Both struck me as outrageous and my tendency to haggle kicked in. I once spent five hours in a Turkish carpet shop consuming endless cups of tea and chain-smoking French cigarettes to dicker down the price of a kilim rug.

I countered the newsman's quoted price and he scoffed, waving his hands as if clearing the air. Several more men shuffled over to contribute their unsolicited opinions, their harsh voices ricocheting about the room. Raised voices in India don't always indicate anger. Indian's have a way of sounding incensed when it's really passion. I first discovered this on a train going to the Taj Mahal when I overheard two men's voices escalate to the point I thought fists would fly. I asked another passenger what the fight was about and he'd said, "It is nothing, madam, they are discussing the color of the moon."

In my fragile state, however, it seemed personal. Them against me. Angry at wasting my time on this stupid suggestion, I joined the roar, shouting "Why couldn't things ever be easy in

India?" and "Who were all these busybody men getting involved?" Our bickering continued, pecking at each other not knowing what the other really said, until I'd had enough and fled the office in tears, muttering, "Dumb, dumb, dumb idea."

12

One Question

Every time I visited the police station to ask about my case, Captain Dutt said, "These things take time, madam." On the third day, I sat on a dusty stone bench under a parched neem tree, waiting to tell Captain Dutt I was leaving Pushkar in the morning and if, by some miracle, the police recovered my items they should notify Patralekha in New Delhi.

"Just fifteen minutes, madam," said a frumpy officer when I asked for the umpteenth time how much longer I had to wait.

Time ticked differently in India, and "fifteen minutes" was never fifteen literal minutes. It's a placeholder or euphemism that in this case could mean, "Go away. We are done with you and your pitiful case."

Hot, thirsty, and feeling abused, I wandered across the road to the row of rickety kiosks in search of a cold drink. I walked along, peering into the wooden booths displaying grimy packets of spicy snacks, tubes of cookies, and sleeping shopkeepers. At the last shop, a swarthy fat man reclined lazy-eyed like a human toad in the corner, swatting flies with a soiled red rag, and I asked for a Thumbs Up cola.

"Cold. I only want a cold one," I said.

"Yes. Cold," he assured, rolling toward an ice chest, extracting one, popping off the cap, and handing me the warm bottle.

The market area offered no relief from the scorching sun and nothing to sit on except a single cinder block. I'd collapsed onto it and was nursing the soda, planning my escape from the dreadful place, when I heard shoes shuffling behind me as the bulky shadow of a male poured over me. I didn't turn around or look up. Didn't need to. The scene was all too familiar. I knew what he wanted.

He hovered over me saying nothing for several beats of my heart before finally uttering in a soft rueful voice, "Excuse me, madam."

Unfooled and unfazed by his tone, I said nothing, only tipped the tepid bottle to my lips while willing him away.

"Madam?" he repeated, "May I ask you one question?"

My mind screamed *NO! A THOUSAND NOS!!!!* Certain, since I was a woman sitting alone, that his question would be, 'Are you married?' or 'Are you alone?' or worse, 'Can I fuck you?' It was as if men in foreign lands, upon seeing me alone with no man to protect my honor, branded me promiscuous. Years ago, in preparation of traveling abroad, I'd bought and wore an inexpensive gold band as a talisman against unwanted advances. But I'd quickly discovered its symbolism meant nothing in cultures that didn't practice the same custom.

I knew what this guy would ask and knew there was no stopping him from asking it.

"*WHAT?*" I said. "What do you want?"

"Madam, did you lose a bag?"

13

The Search

I twisted around and looked up at a stoop-shouldered, teen mildly considering me. He said his name was Mukesh and he was on a bus headed for Ajmer when he and the bus driver saw something fall from my motorcycle. The driver stopped and the two yelled to get my attention, but I'd rounded a curve and disappeared.

"I read the Lost-and-Founds daily, but do not see a posting for a lost bag."

I groaned, remembering the waiter and my frustration at the news office, and muttered, "Stupid."

"Madam?" he asked.

"Nothing. Not you," I said.

Mukesh explained he had spent days searching for a "simple bike," believing it would be easy to find since many foreigners customized their Bullets into Easy-Rider choppers. I hadn't modified Kali much, choosing to keep her in the manufacturer's original condition, except for Nanna's custom-made seat to allow my feet to firmly touch the ground.

"Just now," he said. "I see this bike in front of the police station and you in the courtyard. I wait for the man who must be riding it. I wait and watch for a long time, but no man appears. Then I think, maybe she is the man."

"Where is my bag?"

"I instructed the bus driver to take it home with him. I did not think it safe to leave at the station."

I found it odd, this languid boy giving orders to a man, but Mukesh, a tout, a hustler, possessed other peculiarities too. His tempo wasn't the usual Indian singsong rhythm, it was flat and intoned with a hodgepodge of global accents, assuming the cadence of every tourist simultaneously. As a hotel hustler, he met foreigners at the bus station and escorted them to hotels that paid commissions. His meek presence likely lulled people into following him, but under his boyish persona was a man.

Mukesh refused to walk over to the police station where Kali was parked, mumbling something about past trouble with the police. That didn't surprise or concern me, people who worked the streets had run-ins with the police all the time. I didn't think he was hustling me since he knew about my bag, so I retrieved Kali and, locking my helmet to the rack, rode her over to where he stood.

"Where to?" I asked, as he climbed on behind me.

"Straight," he ordered.

He perched himself rigidly as far back from me as possible and plastered his hands to his thighs. The divide between us unbalanced Kali. Just as I'd been taught to be "one with the motorcycle," Mukesh needed to be "one with me." Instead, his body acted as a rudder, making steering a struggle. I almost asked him to scoot closer, but decided against it. I didn't want to give him ideas.

Kali wobbled as she carried us out of town and between fields of ripening corn, their tassels slumped in the summer sun.

I assumed Mukesh knew where the bus driver lived, assumed he and the bus driver were friends, assumed we were on our way to the bus driver's house as Mukesh shouted directions in my ear.

"Turn here," he instructed, as we neared a crossroad.

"Where exactly are we going?" I shouted back.

"I will tell you as we go."

It annoyed me to be kept in the dark, but I reminded myself that even if he rattled off an address, I couldn't find it on my own. The bike bumped along the rutted road, and the few people walking down the middle of it quickened their pace to get out of the way at the sound of Kali's engine. Focused on getting my stuff back, I didn't realize we'd ridden to Ajmer until Mukesh directed me to turn right and I saw the city bus station.

"I thought you were taking me to the driver's house?" I asked.

"I do not know where he lives," Mukesh said. "I must ask for him at his work. You wait here."

I parked and, ignoring his dictate, followed him into the station where dozens of men in both wrinkled and crisp uniforms shambled between parked buses.

"Shift change," he said, over his shoulder.

We meandered through the group, Mukesh's eyes trolling the lot for the driver.

"I do not see him," he said. "I will have to inquire at the office. You wait here."

I dropped back a bit then followed him into the office, leaning in the doorway while he and an official, sitting at a desk, exchanged words. Mukesh nodded then turned to leave and nearly ran into me.

Startled and annoyed to realize I hadn't obeyed, he curtly said, "Mr. Bakshi is home. Sick."

"Okay, let's go to his home."

"I will try to learn where he lives," Mukesh said. Then, lowering his voice to a whisper added, "Go wait for me by the motorcycle while I chat with these bus wallahs. They do not trust you."

I wanted to argue he was the suspicious one, but I had to admit my appearance caused a stir. Several men had bunched up behind me in the doorway, and I needed to nudge them aside to get out. A few minutes later, Mukesh trotted across the parking lot and hoisted his thick leg over Kali's rear. This time sitting a little closer than before.

"*Chalo*," he announced, insisting I drive.

"Go where? Do you have his address?" I said.

"Follow my directions," he shouted, and my jaw clenched.

Within minutes we escaped Ajmer's traffic, leaving the roiling, rackety city and caustic fumes behind, and were on a country road where sweet, freshly cut grass and overheated dirt, soothing aromas from my childhood, peppered the air. I started to relax, but it didn't last long because the quiet country quickly gave way to a village market. Children squealed and chased each other between weathered carts overburdened with glistening vegetables of every sort and color. Clusters of women perused and pinched tomatoes, okra, and onions as if judges at a county fair.

Mukesh's hands crept from his thighs to my hips when I hit the first of many potholes that salted the road, and I sensed his lips near my ear as he shouted, "Turn left up ahead."

I wondered if his newfound friendliness should concern me. Was he working up to something? Would his hands "slip" higher the next time I inevitably hit another pothole? And if they did, what would I do? I hesitated, not liking confrontation and not wanting to jump to a wrong conclusion. I decided to hold my tongue, reminding myself that his closeness made handling Kali easier by making us one with her.

A flash of color caught my eye as a cow with horns painted pink veered from a *sabzi* wallah's cart, a wad of stolen cilantro sprouting from her mouth. The vegetable vendor hurled rocks at her, and she picked up speed. The market's narrowness and congestion trapped me in her path, and I braced myself for the blow. The cow's boney head slammed into my right hand, smashing my pinky and ripping a chunk from the foam handgrip. Kali wobbled and, in my attempt to prevent toppling over, I shifted too much weight left. The over-compensation disturbed the bike's balance even more, and I lost control, nearly butt-ending an old man as I grappled to stay upright.

"You must be careful," Mukesh admonished, as his hands slid further up my waist.

His hands no longer felt innocent, but I forced the rising grumble in my throat down, saying to myself, *Not now. You need him.*

I regained control and rode out of the village into the countryside again. Mukesh shouted, "Stop here," as we approached a small blue house near a field of wildflowers, hopping off Kali as I halted. Relieved he was no longer behind me and that we'd found the driver's home, I calmed as he jogged toward the porch. A woman in a limp cotton sari stepped out from behind a screen door and the two spoke for some time before he returned and boosted himself back on.

"What are you doing? Isn't Mr. Bakshi home?"

"This is not his home. I am simply getting more directions," he said settling onto Kali, keeping his hands to himself this time.

Mukesh guided me through lanes and neighborhoods for thirty minutes, commanding me to stop here or there to gather more clues to the whereabouts of Mr. Bakshi's house. Everyone we met held some piece to the puzzle. An old man walking toward a field said a bus driver lived in Diggi Bazaar but he did not know his name. In Diggi Bazaar, a shopkeeper said a Mr. Bakshi lived across from the Mahabodhi Mission, but he was unsure if that Mr. Bakshi drove a bus. In Mahabodhi Mission two teenage boys said in crisp English we should ask the sabzi wallah on the corner because "he is knowing everyone." On and on we went, until a group of sweaty boys kicking a ball around pointed to a somber white house teetering at the end of a waterlogged lane and said, "Mr. Bakshi the bus driver is living there."

14

Suspicions

"What do you want?" said a man, stepping through a doorframe painted with a *svastika*—the ancient Hindu symbol for well-being—summoned by the three little girls who'd skittered into the house when I'd said, "Hello." Dressed in undershirts and skirts, the girls peered from behind the man's splayed legs. His harsh tone matched his bear-like eyes. Unaccustomed to being greeted with such hostility, I shifted my feet and wondered if I should speak. Before I could, Mukesh said something I couldn't understand and the man replied in taut English, "My uncle is not home from work," as he remained boulder-like in the doorway. Mukesh spoke again, and this time the man stepped aside and waved us in. I mounted the steps, wondering where Mr. Bakshi was if his family thought he was at work and his employer thought he was home sick. I tried to catch Mukesh's eye to shoot him a raised brow, but he'd tromped ahead as if nothing were amiss.

The man identified himself as Tejas and led us to an area in the home's center, pointing to the string bed to indicate I should sit, then leaned against the wall and stared at me. No doubt I looked a fright from the heat, but the harshness of his reproving expression suggested something else. After a moment or two, his intensity softened and he turned to Mukesh who'd begun speaking in dialect, replaying what I assumed was our lost-and-found story. While they whispered, I surveyed the room and noticed two honey-skinned teenage girls in loose, floral salwar pantsuits clutching each other's forearms as they oscillated in the corner. They giggled and probed me with their liquid bronze eyes, and I lifted the corners of my mouth, hoping to convey solidarity —just another woman making it in a man's world.

A striped curtain sequestered two women in the kitchen. Through the opening I saw them squatting on the floor dicing potatoes and onions, a bag of rice beside them. I guessed the women were mother-in-law and daughter-in-law, as Indian women go to live in their husband's homes. The older woman, clad in a white sari signifying her widowhood, was frail around the shoulders but wide at the hips from childbearing. On her reedy wrists clattered silver bangles, perhaps part of her dowery. The younger woman's weathered hands swiftly and expertly sifted rice searching for pebbles; braided hair, thick as a horse's tail, trailed her spine. Their companionable rhythm soothed me and I wondered if they had a loving relationship or if it even mattered. When the younger woman caught me—a stranger—looking, she pulled her sari's pallu across her face and ordered one of the girls to close the curtain's gap.

I returned my attention to Mukesh and Tejas' conversation. While I still could not understand their words, I thought their tone had taken on a conspiratorial edge. Tejas noticed me listening and switched to English.

"What is it you want with my uncle?"

That took me aback. If they hadn't been discussing my reason for being there, then what had they been talking about?

"Mukesh said he and your uncle found the bag I lost several days ago," I said.

Tejas seemed to tense before saying, "We have a bag, but how can we be sure it is yours?"

That didn't make sense. Did he think Mukesh had delivered an impostor in some ruse to claim it? Or was Tejas engineering some tactic to keep my things? A darker thought entered my mind, maybe my camera and things were crushed in the fall. Maybe a truck ran over the bag before Mukesh and Mr. Bakshi could reach it? Maybe they were stalling rather than tell me. But if that were the case, Mukesh would not have bothered to approach me in the first place. Who wants to be the bearer of such news? It finally occurred to me that Tejas sought some sort of proof that the things were mine.

"I can describe the items," I said.

"No, madam. I did not mean to suggest anything," he said, his expression shifting to deference.

Mukesh, for all his previous chatter, now sat silently at the opposite end of the charpoy. Again, I tried to catch his eye to give him a What's-up look, but he remained stoic. Something was definitely going on, and something had definitely been implied. Why not just hand the bag over? I couldn't understand what kind of charade this might be. None of it made sense.

"My uncle will be home soon. Speak to him then," Tejas said.

I thought that was all he was going to say, but he added, as if coming to some conclusion about me, "I will get your bag now."

I waited for him to go, but he didn't move, so I listed the bag's contents. When I finished, he rose to fetch it. Watching him leave, I wanted to ask Mukesh what was going on, but I didn't dare. I didn't understand the situation, nor did I know who to trust.

15

The Innocence of Guilt

"I can't believe nothing broke," I said, pulling each item from the pack.

Tejas and Mukesh studied me as I removed and inspected the camera and lenses, the Swiss knife, the compass, and guidebook. I thought their eyes brightened at the sight of my journal, and I wondered if they had read it. I tried to recall if it contained anything intimate, but dismissed the concern, figuring they didn't necessarily read English even though they spoke it, and certainly not my handwriting. Besides, once I left their home, I'd never see them again.

When I finished my inspection, I looked up smiling but found Mukesh and Tejas' faces set in grim expressions. Neither said a word. I was about to say something witty to combat their mood when the front door opened and the three of us turned to look.

"Uncle!" Tejas said.

Mr. Bakshi's weary footsteps carried him in, but he stopped abruptly when he saw me. Explanations tumbled out of Tejas as he rousted our little party and ushered us into a sitting room at the front of the house. There, we were introduced. I started to offer my hand to Mr. Bakshi but remembered my place as a woman in this culture when I saw he kept his arms stiff, reminding me that in his traditional home, strangers of the opposite sexes don't touch. I sat on the edge of a plush green sofa and I shoved my hands under my legs, studying Mr. Bakshi's face. Even in the room's sullen light, I detected his troubled demeanor.

I remained on the edge of the sofa while Mukesh languidly reclined on the opposite end. One of the gangly teenage girls hauled in a dining chair for Mr. Bakshi, while Tejas slouched in a corner. Mr. Bakshi, a stoney-faced man with a thatch of hair too thick to be real, spoke to his nephew but kept his eyes riveted on me. Whatever he said, it bolted Mukesh upright.

"He has been most afraid having this bag in his home," Tejas said.

Mukesh's eyes swelled to the size of goose eggs, but he said nothing.

"Every day he travels back and forth looking for a simple motorcycle in hopes of catching the owner. For three days!" Tejas said, his hostility returning. "He is most upset."

I didn't understand Mr. Bakshi's distress or their recriminations. Why were they upset? I'd lost everything. I'd been sickened by the loss. My mind reeled for something to say as Mukesh and the other two carried on as if I didn't exist. I tried to interject, but Mr. Bakshi's waving hands and suddenly excited spirit warned me off. What's the big deal, I wanted to shriek? My eyes burned holes in the back of Mukesh's head, willing him to explain but got nothing. Finally, the men quieted and the weight of their suspicions settled upon me when Tejas asked, "Can you tell us what is in those small pouches hidden in your bag?"

Small pouches? There were no small pouches. There was nothing hidden. The only items in my bag were the ones I'd named earlier.

"What pouches?"

Their eyes sparked and friction crackled the air.

"What pouches?" I insisted, impatient with their tactics.

Mukesh received some telepathic message from Mr. Bakshi, and he reached into the camera case sitting between us, extracting two muslin pouches.

"These," he said, dangling the palm-sized bags before me as evidence of my deceit.

Mr. Bakshi scooted his chair closer.

I stared at the pulpy pouches, knowing what they were but not knowing what they thought they were. The rough cotton bulged with shimmering silicon crystals that kept my camera dry from humidity. I'd forgotten about them. Hadn't imagined them to be anything other than what they were, but then I saw what they saw.

"Drugs? You think these are drugs?" I cried, relief welling in me. They believed I was a drug smuggler. Did they think the pink rocks were crack cocaine? Crystal meth? And why not, weren't all foreigners in Pushkar peddlers? It's one thing to have a little *bhang*, the cannabis concoction juice wallahs mix into yogurt lassis, but the pastel nuggets in my bag represented an ominous outside threat. Their beliefs of foreigners were tainted by hearsay and limited interactions. They knew who I was and what I was capable of based on their belief of all Westerners. But was I guilty of the same misjudgment?

Before leaving New Delhi on this journey, I was warned of the dishonest people I'd encounter along the way—*dacoits* (highway robbers) and cheating hotel clerks, waiters, merchants, mechanics. Friends insisted it was so dangerous that I should carry a gun. At the very least, they'd warned, I'd be taken advantage of because I was a foreigner and a woman. With those messages echoing in me, it was difficult not to see others as unsavory.

Mr. Bakshi, despite his fear and anxiety, however, had kept what he'd believed were illegal drugs in his home—at significant risk to his family and himself—to do the right thing and return the items to the owner. Hearing my explanation of the bag's contents, Mr. Bakshi visibly slumped with relief. The other two grinned.

"Chai. We must celebrate," Tejas ordered, as the teenage girls lurking near the doorway hurried off to fetch it.

काली

Mukesh and I stopped at a bleak family cafe on the ride back to Pushkar, sipping cola and eating chow mein as we faced each other from across the booth. I'd surreptitiously handed Mr. Bakshi several folded hundred rupees as a reward for keeping my belongings safe, and he'd quietly pocketed the money.

"It's a miracle," I said, sliding more money than I'd given Mr. Bakshi toward Mukesh, hoping it was enough. "You finding me. Us finding Mr. Bakshi."

Mukesh beamed and shoved the money into his shirt pocket without glancing at it. A suggestive smile played at the corners of his lips and I saw the bashful boy who'd approached me in the hot sun no longer existed. His shoulders now seemed broader, his chest fuller, and his eyes darker.

"Yes, yes," he said, the tips of his fingers stroking my knee under the table.

I crossed my legs, moving them out of reach. Mukesh, unfazed by my withdrawal, folded his hands on top of the table and continued to marvel over the affair.

"Yes, yes, I know. It is a wonder," he said, reaching across to caress my bare arm.

I slipped it from under his palm and made an elaborate show of picking up my fork to eat more chow mein. I wanted him to get the message without a confrontation, without demanding, "Cut it out."

"You were so careless," he chastised, "allowing that cow to hit us in the marketplace." This time he reached across the table and tousled my hair. I glanced around the crowded cafe to see if others were watching, but the families busied themselves with chatter as they feasted on their food under fluorescent lights.

Each of his fleeting touches announced his entitlement, like waves of foot soldiers breaching foreign territory. I recalled the other males before him who'd believed the same. The boy riding by in the car who shouted "Hey Sexy" as he slapped my 13-year-old bottom while I walked along the road with a friend. I'd giggled with my girlfriend at the "honor" he'd bestowed on me, but inside his branding burned. The 40-something-year-old man in the seat next to me on a flight to California when I was 18 years old, my first solo travel, who'd decided to make himself comfortable by putting his head on my shoulder to sleep. I'd sat paralyzed for three hours afraid to tell the flight attendant of this intrusion, afraid to call it what it was: a violation. The boyfriend's brother-in-law who'd crept up behind me one Christmas Eve as I stood alone at a window looking out at falling snow. He took my solitude in the darkened room as an invitation to run his hand up and down the length of my body, as his wife, children, in-laws, and my boyfriend sat laughing in the next room. I'd endured his touch, unable to breathe or stir, waiting for him to withdraw from the room. Who could I tell about his inappropriateness? And why did I label it inappropriate? Wasn't there a better noun: Assault? Violation? If I told my boyfriend, would he believe me? Would he think his family-man brother-in-law was incapable of such a thing? Would he say I was only twenty-three, I'd misinterpreted the gesture. I'd misunderstood. Or worse, the unspoken but ever-present assumption that I'd invited and encouraged it by not demanding he stop. The brother-in-law would, of course, deny it all. My accusation would stain me, not him. Years later, however, when a man in Egypt approached me asking, "Please, may I fuck you?" I shot him an angry look and stormed away. A year after that, when an Indian man snaked his hand along my backside in a crowded market, I'd cranked his thumb into an unnatural angle as we wordlessly flowed along in a sea of humanity. A few months before leaving on this journey, an Indian teen cycling past me slapped my bottom. I'd chased him down and knocked him off his bike with my heavy purple daypack—the very one I'd lost and found.

Mukesh's face, comported in a dreamy come-hither look, suggested he hoped for more than money. I killed his desire with a dead-eyed stare, watching his idea of hanky-panky shrivel as I stood, towering over him, and walked out to Kali.

Over the Edge

16

Uncertainty

The emptiness of India's Thar Desert pulsed like a warning. People who'd once lived on the strip of land dividing the Rann of Kutch and Little Rann had packed their belongings and walked away, leaving their abandoned huts to sink into the sand. I'd been on the road a week and still wasn't used to riding extended periods, averaging less than an hour in the saddle before my body ached to unfurl. The stretch of highway to Barmer soured into little more than a slash across the wanton land and offered no places to rest. Mile after mile, I followed the frayed ribbon of road through scarred and depleted landscape, encountering only the occasional truck headed in the opposite direction—the drivers hospitably dropping their monster tires off the edge to give me room—the hot air pungent with the smell of rotting animal carcasses.

Eventually, the scabby road bloomed wide and smooth again and I found a "proper restaurant," as the Indians call establishments with indoor dining. Eight or nine men dozed on a bright red porch, incapacitated from the heat. The sound of Kali's engine roused a few. They peered at me as I parked, dismounted, and stripped off my gear before feebly lumbering toward the cafe as if in the final stages of starvation. One man pulled himself up and followed me inside where I found an empty room, void of chairs, tables, and possibly kitchen, that reeked of fresh paint and raw lumber. He summoned a teen to unfold a table and chair for me, as he placed a vase before me with a dusty plastic flower in it.

"Chai, madam?" he asked, his face a forest of whiskers poking from the crevices of his gaunt cheeks.

"Nescafe?" I inquired.

"*Nahin,* madam," he said.

I agreed to chai and asked hopefully about eggs, but sensed the answer would be no again, given the newness of the place.

"*Nahin,* madam," he said, shaking his head no as he went to fetch my chai.

He must have said something to the boy because he brought me packages of English cream-filled cookies and a tube of Indian butter biscuits. I wolfed several of them down before the chai arrived. I didn't eat well on the road, which wasn't surprising since I'd never developed a taste for Indian cuisine. My first year in New Delhi, I'd lived in a furnished *barsati,* a Western-style one-bedroom apartment, with a stone veranda, owned by Mr. and Mrs. Gupta. I'd found the apartment in Gulmohar Park, an enclave for Indian journalists, through an ad in the newspaper. Mr. Gupta was a retired *Times of India* editor-in-chief. I'd survived that first year on hard-boiled eggs and white bread that I toasted on a two-burner countertop hotplate hooked up to bottled gas. During my second and third years in India, I discovered an appetite for tandorri chicken, naan, and *aloo gobi.* In the final few months of my time in the city, Thomas and Luise introduced me to Sunday champagne brunches at the Hotel Oberoi, and eating became a pleasure.

The luxury five-star, sequestered behind stiff hedges and boasting exuberant flowers, was just off one of New Delhi's busiest, noisiest, and most polluted roads. Once a month, a gang of expat friends and I loaded up a taxi and rolled through the scrolling iron gates, entering a world of money and privilege. The room rates started at 8,000 rupees ($160 USD) per night, a sum India's poor lived on for months, but the all-you-could-eat buffet with endless-glasses-of-champagne cost just 450 rupees ($9 USD).

Sizzling, throbbing impoverished India disappeared once inside the hotel, replaced with a hushed world papered in gold and ladened with elegantly draped serving stations covered in crisp, bright linens and weighted with silver trays bearing blueberry scones, banana muffins, buttermilk biscuits, honeydew and cantaloupe, strawberries, grapes, watermelon, bananas, sausage patties and links, strips of bacon, sliced ham, flank steak, hash browns, grits, gravy, eggs Benedict with Hollandaise sauce. Freshly squeezed juices—orange, watermelon, guava, litchi, mango, chickoo, pineapple, pomegranate—shimmered like precious gems from within cut crystal stemware, while rich Arabica coffee, English Breakfast, Darjeeling, and Earl Gray teas awaited to be steeped in bone china cups. Chefs in starched white jackets and towering chef hats stood ready to whip up waffles, pancakes, crepes, and eggs of any style to present on gold-rimmed plates. Waiters trussed up in ruby cummerbunds and turbans fashioned into peacock fans hovered nearby, silently waiting to whisk away the empty plates. I'd sip champagne from a fluted glass, fork the morsels into my ravenous mouth with solid silver cutlery, and dab the corners of my mouth with a buttery-soft napkin, forgetting all about the reality outside the walls.

Sitting alone in the empty restaurant picking at the cookie crumbs with the dusty little plastic flower looking back at me made me long for those Sunday brunches with friends. My journey was barely underway, and I had months to go, but I felt shrouded in loneliness despite being a loner. There was no one I could talk to, commiserate with, or connect. I scribbled in my journal nightly, but things remained unexpressed and bottled up inside me. It wasn't the same as human engagement.

17

Permission

At the end of my seventh day on the road, I checked into a guest house for government officials on the outskirts of Barmer filled with fat officials, whose robust arguments filtered into my dreams that night and manufactured nightmares. Still groggy the next morning and with a headache from the heat, I skipped breakfast and rode Kali to a blighted government building to get permission to visit the village of Neemari. My guidebook described the village as "charming" and said official permission was required from the police because it was on the India/Pakistan border.

The empty parking lot seemed strange, and I thought it might be closed for some holiday (India has around seventy public holidays annually), but a man in his twenties, loitering under a tree, nodded toward a side door.

"Madam needs help?" he asked, following me in and up the stairs.

I ignored him and his oozy aura as I strolled the empty halls, thinking I didn't need this man's help, just some man's permission. All the offices were lifeless except one, where a bleak-looking fellow in a khaki uniform and wearing glasses that comically magnified his eyes looked up as I tapped the doorframe.

"Yes?"

"I'm looking for someone to approve my trip to Neemari."

"All gone," he said, plucking a piece of paper from the stack on his desk and scribbling on it. "Come back Monday."

I wasn't sure if he meant all the permission forms had been taken by others, or if those with the power to approve were gone. Either way, I didn't want to wait until Monday, and said, "I've come a long way to see the village," then added, in hopes of impressing him, "By motorcycle."

I sensed the guy from outside slither into the room. Wanting to make it clear we were not together, I put my helmet on the chair next to me to bar him from sitting. Non-plussed by my territorial act, he rested confidently against a file cabinet behind me, his arm snaking over it.

"Why is it you wish to go to Neemari?" the official asked. "There is nothing there."

Why? Why does a chicken cross the road? Why does a man climb a mountain? Why does a woman ride a motorcycle solo around India? Why does anyone do anything?

I didn't say this, instead, I informed him my guidebook claimed it was a "must-see idyllic village with a picturesque pool." The powerless bureaucrat mulled this over, no doubt weighing my request against the easiest way to get rid of me.

"I cannot give permission. Only boss can. He returns Monday," he said, then added, "If you ask the boss, he will only ask many questions. Simply better to go."

This was a first: an official telling me to disobey the law. I stood to leave when he added, "Take him with you."

"NO," I said, with a force that surprised me. I expected the clerk to argue India's stance on the necessity of a male escort as protection and was prepared to push back. Some years earlier, my friend Melissa and I visited the Jama Masjid in Old Delhi. We were about to climb the minaret's stairs when a guard stopped us. "No madams," he'd ordered. "Not safe." We learned that boys hid in the inky crevasses, touching women's privates as they passed. We'd reasoned unsuccessfully with the guard that women weren't the problem and the boys needed to be cleared out. But he was unswayed, and we were forced to wait for a couple, a man and woman, to come along and ask if we could join them. Now, I equally expected this clerk to insist on an escort, but he surprised me.

"Okay. Go then," he said shrugging and returning his attention to the mound of papers on his desk. "If border patrol catches you, tell them you are lost."

Forty-five minutes later—and as many verses of Jeremiah the bullfrog—I reached Neemari. The "picturesque pool" turned out to be an uninspiring cement swimming pool with brackish water behind a fence choked with weeds and thickets. Near the pool was a yellow water tower a few Indian visitors clambered up for the vista. I followed suit, hoping to be awed by what I found at the top, but the land looked as dismal and forlorn from above as it did below. Disappointed there wasn't more to it, I descended the tower and headed back to town.

The setting sun's waning light painted the desert in lavish pastels. I slowed, savoring the coolness and colors, a gift from the goddess Kali in her role as goddess of time and change. A small village caught my attention. The cluster of four perfectly shaped huts, their walls meticulously constructed of symmetrical sticks and topped with thick, thatched roofs reminded me of an Asian version of Sandy's photos from Germany. The earthen courtyard was polished glassy from thousands of sweepings. I pulled over and listened to the faint twitter of unseen birds lilting on the breeze, refueling my soul until darkness seeped in. On the ride back to town, I reminded myself that beauty revealed itself in unexpected ways and places—if I kept my mind open to it.

काली

The monsoons hadn't reappeared since my first day, yet evidence of storms surrounded me. I crossed four swollen rivers and ten ponds overflowing into the road, each encounter growing feelings of accomplishment.

Heavy rains had carried away most of an old bridge on my way to Mount Abu. In its place, a vast, new cement beast yawned over a swiftly flowing ravine. Although I couldn't see all the way across, it appeared finished to me, even though men and women continued mixing cement. I got halfway and stopped, Kali's engine slowing to a soft growl, as the men shouted and pointed.

I'd slipped past them while they were busy mixing cement and now their thin angry voices chased me in the sticky air. In my rearview mirror, I saw they'd abandoned their work and were coming toward me—their brown torsos shiny with sweat, their arms gesticulating and pointing. My eyes followed the direction of their urgency. A detour along a muddy hillside. A slick of viscous earth, evidence of the monsoons that spelled treachery. A slender knife-edged cut into a soggy mound. A track not fit for goats. On its glassy surface, a man on a scooter fishtailed violently, spewing an arc of wetness into the air behind him.

The leathery women working alongside the men laid down their cement pans and silently joined the men on the bridge. Their skirts, like the men's lungis, were tucked between their legs to create pantaloons. Their once bright blouses and ropy limbs were dusted and dulled with fine gritty cement. The men bellowed and gestured at the hillside, insisting I get off the bridge, insisting I take the detour.

No way, not when there was a bridge to the highway.

"*Nahin, nahin*," I shouted, shaking my head. "This way."

They shook their heads back, demanding I take the other path. We waggled our heads at each other until they gave in and waved me on. A smile twitched at the corners of my mouth as I twisted Kali's throttle. But, I didn't get far. The bridge was unfinished. Between me and the highway lay five feet of imposing gully, choked with branches, logs, and stones that Kali could not cross.

I stared at the blockage, willing a way to cross it to appear. When it didn't, I considered turning back, but the construction workers blocked the way. I heard a familiar little voice inside insisting, *"Prove it. Prove it. Prove it."*

I found the least dangerous, flattest spot in the bramble and eased the clutch out. Kali snarled as her tires chewed into the debris, churning obstacles aside as she sought purchase. Together, we neared the highway, success inches away. Then, her front tire snagged on a root and her heavy front end snapped hard to the left. The force reverberated through me, pinging in me like an electrical jolt. I jammed my foot into the ground, stiffened my arms, and threw all of my 120 pounds into keeping the 500-pound motorcycle upright. My mind shrilled, *"No, no, no, no, no,"* as Kali inched lower to the ground. My arms burned as the earth swallowed my foot and my grip gave way. I pleaded, *"please, please, please."*

Just as I was sure I'd lose, Kali righted and we bounded over the barrier, bouncing onto the road. Tempted to look back triumphantly, but not wanting to tempt fate more, I kept my eyes looking forward as I sped toward Mount Abu.

18

Birth of a Goddess

A series of sweeping bends embraced Mount Abu—the honeymoon capital of India—like piping on a wedding cake, with thin shafts of sunlight dancing on the road. I still reveled from my success at the bridge earlier, and I planned to reward myself with a few days watching cable television at a sumptuous hotel in Mount Abu, venturing out only to discover which piece of the goddess fell to earth at my second shakti peetha temple site.

The switchback up the mountain was nothing like my first experience riding Kali up a mountain, on my way to Mussoorie to study Hindi prior to this journey. I'd traveled alongside Endo, a Japanese Communist journalist friend, on a flat and fine road that corkscrewed at the base of the mountain then clogged into a series of pinched turns at the center of the hillside town. No one —including my guru mechanic Nanna—warned me to adjust Kali's idle to enrich the mixture of fuel and oxygen that riding in higher altitudes required. By the time I reached the town's heart, Kali was sputtering and dying over and over, as I zig-zagged around pedestrians percolating between shops, leaving me wrestling hundreds of pounds of steel on the steep street. Endo had ridden ahead of me and wasn't aware of my predicament. By the time I made it through town, I could barely ride, as frustration roiled through me. But then, things got worse.

At the mountain's top raged a storm. The pouring rain transformed the road into a river, making it barely visible. Drenched and freezing in the cold mountain air, my teeth chattered as I careened perilously close to the edge on a hairpin turn.

The ride to Mount Abu didn't compare to that trip. I now knew to adjust Kali's idle before entering a different altitude, and it was dry and sunny. But it took ten hours to ride the 183 miles, and I arrived at the Sunrise Palace Hotel depleted.

The former maharaja's summer retreat retained its air of royalty, even though the prince's personal belongings were replaced with cheap imitations and sitar-strumming musicians with cable television. I planned to watch *The X-Files* after scrubbing the road off myself and finding some food. The shower (no bucket bath) rejuvenated me with hot stinging needles that soothed my muscles. I changed into my remaining clean items—my nightly laundry ritual had severely lapsed. Noting I'd have to deal with it before descending the mountain, I loped onto the streets to find food. Mount Abu offered plenty of restaurants, and I discovered fried chicken and sautéed vegetables at a lively place where a waiter with kind eyes smiled as he delivered my favorite foods. I walked back to the hotel feeling satisfied under a bruised twilight sky, marveling at the giant fruit bats spiraling in search of their dinner.

I woke late the next day to waterlogged air, as a dense fog smothered the land and turned the outside world into a murky mystery. At the front desk, I arranged for my clothes to be laundered and asked for directions to Adhar Devi Temple, my second shakti peetha temple. Along the path, I repeatedly stumbled over roots and mistook trees for people, offering them excuses. I was alone on the ascent and it wasn't until I heard voices that I realized I'd reached the temple. Except there was no temple, only an entrance to a cave with a sign declaring: *Cameras, radios, and sticks are not allowed in the temple.*

Since losing and finding my backpack, I'd not let it out of my sight and contemplated ignoring the rule until I felt the attendant's eyes on me and handed it over. He proffered a gold token bearing a number in return and placed my bag on a low shelf along with an identical coin.

The redolent scent of cool, moist earth rushed my senses, and I flashed back to a cave in the Czech Republic that I thought I'd die in. I was a novice caver in college, cautiously exploring Central Indiana's karst riddled terrain on the weekends with friends. When one of the men I'd interviewed for a caving story for the *Prague Post* invited me to join him one weekend, I'd accepted.

Ctirad took me and a teenage boy he'd brought along to a well-explored cave and handed me the only helmet with a headlamp, along with one of the three flashlights. I knew we each needed a helmet with a headlamp and two more light sources to be safe. But we'd driven so far, and the thought of attempting to communicate my reluctance to the two who didn't speak much English seemed impossible. Besides, I didn't want to be a spoilsport and I convinced myself it would be okay.

The cave's entrance was a hole in the ground, and we single-filed in behind Ctirad, chimney-walking ourselves down into it by pressing our backs and legs against opposite sides. The acrid smell of guano whistled past me as the cave softly breathed. We belly-crawled then stoop-walked through the cave's intestinal tracks for what seemed like hours before plundering upon a yawning pit at the bottom of a cold, thirty-foot steel ladder. Once we were all down on the ballroom's slick floor, we doused our lights, as tradition dictates among cavers, plunging ourselves into a darkness so black only deep space rivaled it. My mind flailed in the space, solid and devoid of any light, struggling to make out any familiar shape before relinquishing myself to a primordial state-of-being, one only experienced in a mother's womb. It was thrilling, unnatural, and deeply disturbing.

The passages leading away from the ballroom pinched into veins pounded out by centuries of water that ate away the rock. We sluiced ourselves through them, penetrating deeper and deeper into Mother Nature, arriving at the cave's end, a slimy little cubbyhole equipped with a slack rope ladder dangling over a ledge's lip. Feeling brave, I climbed it, hoping to be rewarded with some of the cave's jewels, perhaps a pink quartz rosebud peeping from under a ledge or a few delicate soda straws refracting in my headlamp's light.

As a kid, I scaled the linen closet to peek inside the delicate boxes at the top containing my mother's jewelry. My little fingers of one hand clung to the shelves as I stretched on tippy toes to lift the lids with the other. Inside the dime-store boxes rested my mother's emerald necklace, her diamond-studded bee broach, and her string of pearls, each on a cotton square. They weren't real or valuable to anyone but me. To me they signified reward. Success at having scaled the impossible.

As I neared the top of the cave's rope ladder, I was stricken with a certainty that something was terribly wrong. My body, or rather butt, hung too far out over the cave's floor. The rope ladder collapsed, spitting me off it like a cherry pit. My hands ripped from the rope as my body arched backward. But instead of thrashing and panicking, I grew strangely calm and unafraid. Time suspended. I tumbled backward then upside down. My body and mind uncoupled. I witnessed myself plummeting as if watching a film in slow motion, each incremental inch of my descent freeze-framed into stills. Marionette-like, I observed parts of my body—head, neck, right shoulder, left shoulder, right then left hip—slam into the cool earth. Breath, not life, was jettisoned from me. I lay stunned on the bedrock floor, unable to inhale. Nothing was broken except my confidence. The helmet saved my life. I opened my eyes and saw Ctirad's concerned expression regarding me. It was the same expression I saw on my motorcycle instructor's face when I crashed during my training course, and one I'd see again on the face of a stranger standing over me as I lay on a charpoy recovering from a crash on a desolate highway in southern India.

काली

I hesitated at the temple-cave's mouth, rationalizing it wasn't dangerous if elderly women in saris and children munching popcorn trotted in and out. Stooping, I stepped into the slender passage that lead to the main hall. Dozens of miniature, clay oil-filled vessels were nested on the cave's natural ledges, bathing it in a frail, pulsing glow. The chamber was shallow, and along the back towered a statue of Durga—the demon slayer draped in a cockeyed, yellow satin cape—one of Kali's many incarnations. A silver tray piled with offerings of flower petals, coconut slivers, rupee notes, and a scattering of coins rested at her feet, along with a plaster lion. It was Durga's *vahana*, her vehicle. Each god and goddess has their own manner of transportation (Ganesh, the elephant-headed god rides a rat). The tawny big cat's frozen snarl revealed white fangs and a long red tongue.

I didn't notice the priest sitting in the shadows, one leg curled beneath him, but he spotted me and waved to the cushion next to him. I eased myself down, hoping this wouldn't take long. I didn't like caves and was beginning to think I didn't like temples either. I went to church as a kid, collecting a couple of years' worth of perfect-attendance pins, and envied an old man whose dedication pins tumbled down the length of his body, but I wasn't religious. In Europe, I visited the world's most famous churches, browsing them as if they were museums rather than in the pursuit of God's spirit. India's temples felt even more spiritually remote to me. I was there for one reason only: to collect another piece of the Mother Goddess.

I smiled at the priest, a heavyset man in his thirties, wondering how long I should sit with him before asking my question. I was losing my ability for conversation. In the few weeks I'd been on the road, I'd increasingly retreated into the noise in my own head; my last real conversation with friends in New Delhi little more than a warm fading memory. Now, my exchanges centered on room requests and meal orders. The priest smiled and told me his family had served as priests of the temple for eight generations. He lived next to the temple with his mother, six brothers, their wives, and children. I listened politely, but offered nothing in return, waiting for a lull so I could ask what I really wanted to know. When it came, he responded by tapping his full mouth with a red-stained forefinger, the one he used to dab vermillion onto the foreheads of worshipers as a blessing, and said, "Lips."

19

One of Them, Only Different

It took six days for my clothes to dry in Mount Abu's moist air, before I headed back to the Thar Desert, where temperatures normally clocked in at 122 degrees Fahrenheit, zapping my energy and swelling my lips. I forgot to adjust Kali's front brakes for the descent, and was forced to ride in second gear while keeping pressure on the rear brake. The changing altitude that on the ascent had ballooned the tires now deflated them, so I pulled into a garage for some air and had the attendant adjust the brakes, feeling too lazy to dig out my mechanical notes to do it myself.

Bhuj was my day's destination, but the roads were so rough and shattering, my insides ached. Averaging nineteen-miles an hour, it took me a grueling six hours to cover 114 miles, less than halfway to Bhuj. By 2 p.m., I was ready to quit for the day and stopped on the side of the road to check my map for a town large enough to offer a hotel or guesthouse.

Radhanpur seemed my best bet and I followed the signs to it and ran into a crowd waiting at a train barrier. I pulled in behind them and switched off Kali. More villagers bunched behind me. Smothered in denim and leather and topped with a shiny black full-faced helmet, I was a beacon of strangeness among a sea of men in flowing white garments.

Shoulder to shoulder in the bundle of sweaty men, no air stirring, and no sign of when the train would pass, I peeled off my gloves. It's impossible to imagine the men could get any closer but they somehow did as they swiveled their heads to gawk.

I tugged my jacket off next, and the men tightened around me more, as those in the back pushed to get a better look. But when I removed my helmet, instead of getting closer, they backed away. The sight of a woman alone on that motorcycle jolted them into retreating. The rift in their sea allowed a band of nomadic women to move in closer, their faces, inked in blue stars and triangles, riveted with curiosity.

They trickled toward me, leaving the sheep they herded across scorched land blinking and unattended. Life had hardened the women and they appeared ancient and otherworldly, yet somehow girlish. They giggled and tittered, tentatively reaching weathered calloused hands out to touch me. Pushing their stenciled and pierced faces close to mine, I felt their warm breath on my skin as one or two gently stroked my fair hair. Its downy texture like gossamer in their hardened hands before they compared it to their own course strands. Delighted, they caressed my overheated cheeks and pinched my shrunken breasts before touching their leathery skin and hefting their plump breasts at me as if to say, "What happened to yours?"

As the women swirled around me—the men blinking like the sheep on the periphery—their heavy silver bangles clattered musically on their wrists and ankles. Oscillating like mystic creatures, they shrieked at their discoveries.

It wasn't the first time in my travels other women behaved this way. In Cairo, Egypt, a troupe of ladies approached me at a musical recital during Eid al-Adha—the Muslim festival involving fasting and celebration that marks the pilgrimages to Mecca. They too compared our bodies; I'd been startled and intimidated by their intrusive pawing. But there was something different about my encounter with these nomadic Indian women. They were wild birds. They recognized that the woman before them, one of them only different, needed their connection—needed to grasp that despite her isolation she was not alone. I savored their velvety touches as they withdrew and returned to their flock. For miles, I felt the comforting warmth of their rough hands on my starved soul.

20

Ladies of a Different Order

B huj did not fit the expectations I drew from the description in my guidebook as "a place out of a Rudyard Kipling book." My mind conjured up an image of a quaint, time-forgotten village but instead, I found a writhing, modern desert town teeming with dry-goods stores, chemist shops, and ice cream parlors. Trucks, cars, and motorcycles rumbled past crowds of shoppers. The dizzying activity was disorientating after days in the desert. Groups of women promenading freely and unescorted by men popped in and out of ice cream parlors. Indian women didn't operate motor vehicles in New Delhi but in Bhuj, schoolgirls toting girlfriends zipped past fearlessly on scooters. Both women and girls exuded confidence and independence their interior sisters lacked.

The town was gearing up to celebrate India's 50th anniversary of autonomy from British rule, and bright buntings, banners, and tinsel festooned the shopfronts. I'd been on the road for sixteen days and had covered less than 1,000 miles—miles riders in the United States covered in twenty-four hours as part of the Iron Butt Association's challenge. My butt didn't hurt but my shoulder blades and muscles in my upper back were knotted from riding on rutted roads and dodging manic drivers.

I'd checked into a hotel and was now on a mission to find a hot water bottle for my aching back. Weaving through the shoppers in search of a chemist shop, I encountered an obstruction. A Brahmin bull, the size of a Mini Cooper, lay folded across the sidewalk with a man sitting next to it combing the animal's prodigious head. Behind the man stood a boy combing the man's head. I assumed it was part of the celebratory preparations and wanted to ask someone but before I could a cluster of ladies fenced themselves around me. At first, I thought I'd inadvertently gotten swept up in their group, but realized it wasn't an accident. I steadied myself for another round of petting, but they didn't touch me, only leaned in leeringly.

They were big-boned and thick-muscled, reminding me of refrigerators stuffed into faded floral salwar kameezes and saris. The leader pressed her pulpy face inches from mine, peeping at me with pygmy eyes rimmed in black *kajal* makeup. Her hot tainted breath, a combination of sweet paan and rotten teeth, assailed my nose. Her closeness revealed a slather of thick foundation camouflaging a rash of stubble and I realized she was a he. A *hijra*, a eunuch—meaning 'neither male nor female'—was a third sex. They were part of India's subculture and their unverified population was anywhere from 50,000 to 1.25 million. Traditionally, they danced at weddings and births, their presence considered a blessing at these events for centuries because of the special powers they were believed to possess.

I'd encountered hijras before. Two came to Thomas and Luise's new apartment while they moved in. Luise and I were unpacking dishes and cutlery from boxes when they strolled in the back door wanting to be paid for blessing the house. Such benedictions were accepted practices in Indian society, and at first, they were fun and jokey. But when the money didn't materialize fast enough, they soured, obviously threatening to curse the house as they backed us against the counter. One of the hijras surveyed the kitchen in a way that made me worry she was searching for a weapon, and my blood chilled. Luise scrounged up some money and the pair eventually left, leaving us both with wobbly legs.

The Bhuj hijras terrified me more, the way they quietly contemplated me. I didn't know what they wanted since there was nothing for them to bless. The leader thumped her chest with a manly hand and proclaimed "Dimple," as her girls crushed closer. They were tweaking on something and reeked of testosterone and frankincense.

"You come. Make much," Dimple said, blood-red spittle flinging at me. Paan stained her gums and teeth so that the inside of her mouth looked like a crime scene, reminding me of the horror stories I'd heard about hijras' castrations involving strings, knives, restraints, and hot sticks. I cast around for someone on the street to intervene, but most moved on about their own business.

Of the five hijras, two didn't speak or touch me. They stood back while the other three whirled and howled around me like dervishes. Two of them seized my arms, holding me in place, while Dimple swiveled luridly in front of me, erotically hitching up her sari, threatening to expose what I feared were her mutilated genitals.

"LET GO," I shouted, struggling to free myself from the women's grips, but they held tight.

"Suck. Suck," Dimple teased, lustily poking her finger in her mouth to illustrate her meaning.

My plight now caught everyone's attention. All stared, some laughed, but none moved to help. Dimple and the two flanking me danced vigorously around me on virile feet wedged painfully into delicate, glittery sandals.

"Breast. Breast," Dimple said, pressing near and cupping her flat chest as I fought to back away. "You come. Make much."

I shook my head emphatically, sending a pleading look at the bystanders to save me. Dimple didn't like this, and she glared at them and me with hard hateful eyes. Her contemptuousness caused several of the onlookers to scurry off. Dimple continued insisting I come with them on their rovings, as my mind searched for a way to escape.

One of the hijras noticed my camera bag slung over my shoulder, and chimed, "Photo! Photo!" Like Bollywood divas, the prospect of being preserved in film overcame their desire to torment me. The two squeezing my arms relinquished their hold and pranced to join the others lined up before me as I extracted my Nikon. They giggled, smoothed their outfits, and pinched their manly jowls into radiant bloodspots of cheer and health.

Dimple refused to join them and sulked off-camera, scowling with disapproval. I fiddled around with the camera settings, taking my time in hopes that whatever caused them to seize me dissolved now that Dimple had separated from her pack. My stall worked; whatever Dimple had concocted evaporated as I clicked several frames of the preening quartet. She tromped off down the street and soon her girls followed suit, in search of their next victim. With the show over, the crowd lost interest too, and I was left alone in the bright sunshine to collect my traumatized self.

I needed a drink, but the best I could find was cane-juice from a stall at the end of the road. The juice wallah hand-cranked stiff stalks of succulent cane through a medieval contraption that dribbled golden juice into a tall glass. Watching the juice fill the glass, I didn't notice the grizzled old man hobbling toward me. Crooked and dressed in a starched white kurta, he trundled up grinning at me.

"*Namaste*," he said, bowing and tenting his crooked fingers into steeples. He held the formation high above his head to illustrate his respect for me.

Finally, I thought, a friendly face and returned his greeting on a more modest scale.

"London?" he inquired, nodding with obvious pleasure at guessing correctly.

I've known American travelers who've refused to admit their nationality when abroad, for fear of being treated poorly because of the United States' politics. Instead, they'd claimed to be Canadian, and some went so far as to sew a Canadian flag on their packs. But I never understood the practice. I believe people related to people and not politics. So, I didn't hesitate to tell the old man, "American," sure this would please him since India was celebrating fifty years of independence from Great Britain after 350 years of oppressive rule.

"Amereekaan?" the old man exclaimed, his mouth twisting as if tasting something nasty. "Aaaamerrrrreekaan?" he repeated with disgust. He then fashioned his gnarly hands into guns and began firing at me. "Ratatattat, ratatattat, ratatattat. Amereekaan. Amereekaan," he sneered, spitting on the ground to punctuate his opinion. "No good. No good. America help Pakistan. Guns Pakistan. No good. NO GOOD."

Horrified, I glanced around, praying this wouldn't turn into another street spectacle as his imaginary bullets rained over me. What was wrong with him? I wanted to shout back that I hated war, but didn't. I just stood there absorbing the abuse.

"NO *namaste*. NO *namaste*," he growled, spit on the ground again, and walked away.

Attacked twice in a matter of minutes was more than I could handle. I wanted to lock myself in my hotel room and sleep off the experiences. The juice wallah handed me my drink then twirled a finger around his temple, and apologetically said, "*Pagal*," indicating the man was mad. But I wondered if he was; who's to say he wasn't justified? I am, after all, a piece of a larger puzzle. I have a voice in what my government does, and, by doing or not doing something, I'm accountable.

I gulped the cane juice and walked back to my room, physically and emotionally pained, reminded of something that happened to me in Cairo in 1992 when a wave of terrorist tension washed over Egypt. Attacks on tourists were carried out by bombing the National Museum, a German tour bus, a luxury train, and cafes frequented by foreigners. I was walking down a busy street in Cairo when a young man shoved into me, hissing, "I should kill you." Although a white Westerner in a brown world, I'd never been openly vilified for what I represented until then. I hadn't considered how hated Americans could be in some countries. No matter what was in the old man's mind and heart, I doubted it was as straightforward or simple as the American government supplying arms to Pakistan. There is always something larger going on.

21

Therapy

I laid low for a few days after my encounter with Dimple and the old man, treating myself to restorative beauty treatments of detoxification and exfoliation at Dinki's Beauty parlor. When I lived in New Delhi, I got facials every few weeks from a cramped parlor in the shopping complex where I bought eggs and bread near my house in Gulmohar Park. Dinki's, despite being a one-woman operation, was significantly larger than the shop I enjoyed in New Delhi. There, a team of ladies squeezed into a room half the size of Dinki's expertly applied fresh fruits and vegetables to my face, massaging me with orange slices sprinkled with sugar to open my pores, before splashing me clean with rosewater made from petals soaking in a bowl, to calm my angry skin. They'd smoothed thick, creamy yogurt onto my cheeks, forehead, chin, and nose to tighten my skin. Chilled cucumber slices were placed on my eyes to de-puff them and honey dabbed on my lips to heal them. The first time I got a facial and saw the tray filled with little dishes of fruit and yogurt, I thought lunch came with the pampering.

Dinki used none of these ancient Ayurvedic beauty treatments, instead she poured pre-packaged lotions from pretty bottles. I missed the girls from Gulmohar Park, the energy they exuded filled the shabby little shop and their chatter competed with Indian soap operas blaring from a television in the front room occupied by the fat man who took the money. Dinki's treatment cost twice as much and didn't feel half as good in her sterile environment, but it was still a deliciously soothing antidote to my recent days.

As I exited Dinki's, I was greeted by a sky tinctured in pinks and purples and decided to top off the day by treating myself to an ice cream. I found the King Kone Ice Cream shop at the edge of town, ordered a Drumstick, and plopped back onto Kali to watch a cow feasting on who-knows-what.

As I contemplated the cow's diet, a woman rushed toward me grinning and gesticulating. Her rapid speech made it impossible to detect her language. When she realized I wasn't getting it, she whirled and hurried back to a man sitting on the scooter and tugged him toward me. He smiled meekly and explained, "My wife wants to know if you will come to our house?"

I used to be invited into homes often—in every country—but hadn't been since leaving New Delhi. This couple appeared guileless, and the beauty treatment and ice cream had alleviated some of yesterday's woes, but I wasn't sure about going into their home; my people-radar senses seemed to be on the fritz. Yet this woman, whose name I learned was Ahana, meaning "inner light," radiated goodness. Surely I wasn't wrong about her?

I told them my name and Ahana practiced saying Connie, rolling it along her tongue as if savoring a piece of candy. She pronounced it "Coney," like the island off Manhattan, while Rushil, her husband, smiled demurely.

Ahana began tugging me toward their home, a plain-faced apartment block, dotted with dark windows shuttered for the night. *Whoa,* I thought, *slow down.* Ahana sensed my hesitation and tugged at Rushil's shirtsleeve, an expression of angst scrawled across her pretty features. I explained I was tired and suggested I visit them the next day. Rushil translated this to Ahana, who nodded vigorously, her eyes bright in anticipation. We agreed upon 6 p.m. and Rushil jotted the apartment number on a piece of paper before leading Ahana away, like a child reluctant to leave her best friend.

22

A Family Affair

The next day, I parked Kali in front of their apartment and climbed four flights of gritty stairs, sand blown in from the desert, to Ahana and Rushil's cozy apartment. The front door stood wide open, so I poked my head inside and saw Rushil sitting on a sofa watching television with two little girls snuggled against his sides, the three of them giggling. I knocked and he looked up, surprised to see me. His expression meant one of three things: the invitation had been a perfunctory cultural gesture and I wasn't expected to show up at all; they didn't believe I'd come and weren't prepared for my visit; or they didn't expect me to arrive at 6 p.m. sharp because it's culturally acceptable in India to be two or three hours late. I'd surprised them by being a punctual American.

Rushil sprang off the couch with genuine joy, leaving the kids to collapse into the space he'd evacuated.

"Coney! Please, come in."

Showing good manners, I slipped off my boots and entered the home, glancing at the girls who beheld me with saucer-sized eyes. Ahana heard my voice and hustled in, her arms flung wide as she rushed toward me, wrapping me in a tight hug. It was the most exuberant welcome I'd ever experienced, as most Indians were friendly but not touchy. She hugged and kissed both my cheeks enthusiastically, then hugged me again before taking my face into her hands and gazing at me with love and warmth.

Pointing to the taller of the two girls, now huddled together on the couch, she said, "Kira and Sahana." Six-year-old Kira, whom they called Angel, had her father's candy-sweet eyes and reticent smile. Her blue-black hair was cut in a saucy bob and she twisted the hem of her dress, a wide-collared costume with appliquéd roses. I smiled at her as she clambered off the couch and shrank behind Rushil's legs.

Four-year-old Sahana looked at me as if she were about to burst, her ribbons of coal curls quivered as her eyes pranced and beamed like her mother's. They called her Queenie, and her entire body wriggled with energy on the verge of mischief and delight.

Ahana, embarrassed that I arrived before she'd cleared the room of the girls' things, giggled and swooped, snatching up storybooks, crayons, and dolls. Queenie trotted after her mother pretending to steer a baby buggy while keeping "see-me eyes" trained on me. Angel remained rooted at Rushil's side. Her reaction was the more common one I got from Indian children, who sometimes cried because of my whiteness if I got too close. Once a baby peed on me out of fear. Queenie, however, skipped a little closer to me each time she rounded the room.

Ahana dispatched Rushil to the store for sweets and deposited me on the couch while she finished picking up the room. With her daddy gone, Angel took refuge in the doorway. But watching her younger sister dance dangerously near me as she circled the room inspired her to join Queenie's intrepidness and a game of competitive bravery ensued.

Rushil returned with a delivery boy in tow, both their arms bursting with gooey goodies. The sight of the treats stirred the girls into a greater frenzy, and they forgot about me and skipped into the kitchen after their father. Ahana followed them and emerged with a large tray loaded with the family's favorites: fluted dishes of vanilla ice-cream sprinkled with pistachios and dribbled with cherry syrup, a platter of chocolates wrapped in gold and silver foil, a bowl of spicy *namkeen*, and several bottles of Thumbs Up cola. Thrusting one of the melting ice creams into my hands, she insisted, "Eat. Eat." Rushil smiled at his wife, then at me, and I got the feeling he was never in charge.

When everyone had a sweet, Ahana burst into questions that Rushil translated. She wanted to know where I was from and about my family. He relayed to her that I was in India alone and I had one brother. Her brow crinkled with fissures.

"*Akēlā?*" she asked, over and over, wanting to know if I was alone and shocked to learn I was, especially since I was so far from home. Rushil, a government man, giggled and glanced lovingly at his daughters spooning their way to the bottom of their dishes as if racing. It was odd to hear a man giggle, but it somehow suited him.

"My wife wants to know if you have your brother's permission?" he asked.

The question startled me, although it shouldn't have since India was holistically patriarchal and male permission was still a galling fact for many women. But hearing Ahana ask surprised me. She struck me as a modern woman with modern ways and ideas—and she clearly wore the family pants.

I considered Ahana's question, unsure of how to answer. How horrifying would it be to her for me to say I didn't need my brother's permission? That he wasn't watching over me, thank you very much.

Raksha Bandhan or *rakhi* was in a few days—a celebration of a brother's promise to protect his sister that involves her plying him with sweets and tying a rakhi, a band of colorful thread adorned with decorations, to his wrist.

But maybe my assumption of what was at the heart of her question was wrong? Maybe, like the women in the back of that truck in New Delhi who'd delightedly nudged each other when it dawned on them that the motorcyclist trailing them was a woman, Ahana would be thrilled by my independence. "American women don't need their brothers' permission to go and do. They can do whatever they please," I said, knowing it was a lie. Scores of American women were trapped in controlling relationships.

"*Nahin* permission?" she said, her mouth slightly agape. She wore a blue salwar kameez with bold geometric patterns, a defiant break from the traditional floral designs most women wore. Earlier, she'd brazenly flipped her dupatta over her shoulder, but now her hands clutched the cloth, balling it tight as she leaned in, her expression hungry for more.

I attempted to explain American women's quest for equality and freedom, that thousands of women before me had fought for the rights I now enjoyed, but complicated cultural ideas don't translate well. I didn't want her or Rushil to be concerned for me, so I told them that my family supported my journey, which was true. My mother, although she'd never do any of the things I did, always encouraged me to live my life on my terms and never complained about my choices. After my father died, she could have become clingy, fearful of letting her children far from her side. But that wasn't her way. She wanted her children to soar on their own, confident that was the only way to keep them close and coming back home.

When Rushil told Ahana I had my family's blessing, the tension drained from her face and she grinned as Rushil chortled nervously.

We returned our attention to our forgotten ice creams—mine now a puddle of colors at the bottom of the dish. After a few moments of silence, Ahana had another question.

"My wife wants to know if everyone in America lives on a ranch? Like *Dallas*." Rushil said.

I smiled and lied yes, knowing it would be a long night.

23

Oh Brother, Brother Day

Ahana insisted I join them for Raksha Bandhan, as she dutifully visited her brothers' homes. Dressed in my finest—a wrinkled purple T-shirt, baggy cargo pants, and a tired, frail scarf I'd bought in Italy tied in my hair—I took an autorickshaw to their home the following day. We all then climbed into a waiting taxi where the smell of stale bygone bodies mingled with our fresh soapy scents. Ahana nudged Rushil and me into the back, a place of privilege, then scooted the girls and herself into the front.

The highway was clotted with cars filled with duty-bound families, and we bumped along the brittle road. Angel and Queenie squirmed around to peek at me before burying their faces into the taxi's well-worn cloth. Ahana twisted around chattering, telling me what to expect, while Rushil translated her narrative. First, we would visit her oldest brother and then her baby brother, where her mother lived. Because Ahana and Rushil differed so from other Indian families I knew in New Delhi, I happily anticipated meeting her equally progressive family.

In the spirit of the day, and despite my opposition to the archaic meaning of the rakhi—to literally tie oneself to a man—I decided to give one to Rushil, making him my "honorary brother" as a gesture of my sisterhood with Ahana. This, I hoped, removed me from being a sexual threat to her marriage, given that she watched *Dallas*, with its wanton women.

I presented Rushil with a simple red rakhi made of gold and silver threads and encrusted with a miniature shell medallion, along with a Cadbury candy bar. He snickered as I tied the fragile threads around his proffered wrist. I'd agonized the night before in choosing the right rakhi; one too gaudy or too plain might send an unintended message. This one had seemed right when I bought it, but now appeared appallingly inadequate—even borderline insulting, it was so small. I cringed inside and found it difficult to meet his or Ahana's eyes, but she squealed delightedly and clapped her hands. "Now he brother," she said in English. I'd suspected she spoke some of it but lacked the confidence to use it, much like my Hindi. She reached into her purse and extracted 200 rupees and waved it at Rushil who timidly passed it to me. I nodded and thanked him and her, saying, "*Dhan'yavād.*"

We arrived at Ahana's older brother Sai's home—a free-standing square block on a weedy plot of sand—during a brownout, so the fans weren't stirring. He led us into a living room stuffed with matching brown velveteen furniture that suggested money but, in the overheated house, felt oppressive. Scattered around the room were half a dozen vases containing plastic flowers. Sai grunted and glanced at me as Rushil introduced us, then dismissed my existence by never looking at me again.

"Sit," Rushil said, giggling as he indicated a chair by the door.

An anemic breeze crawled through the open door as I sat feeling like the last doll left on a shelf at a county fair. Sai and his wife Ishita interrogated Rushil and Ahana about me, and I heard

Rushil say, "Bullet" and "Dilly" (meaning Delhi) and list the areas I'd told them I planned to ride.

Square-faced, pointy-eyed Ishita stared at me from across the room, her contemptuous expression rivaling the Wicked Witch of the West. I could almost hear the sharp thoughts cutting across her mind: *What kind of filthy woman rides a filthy motorcycle? A dirty whore. What kind of filthy family lets their filthy daughter do this? A family of dirty whore mongers.*

Ishita's disgusted glare informed me that my efforts to spruce up failed miserably. The purple and black scarf I'd tied artfully around my head that morning now seemed like a fool's undertaking to hide my shaggy unkempt hair, the garment's tattered ends beacons of poverty. I became painfully aware of my frayed collar and threadbare pants. I felt like a vagrant she'd sidestep on the streets. Yet, here I sat on her prized furnishings like something carried in on the bottom of a shoe.

I attempted to make myself less loathsome by widening my eyes in doll-like innocence, sitting taller, and tucking my dirty boots (still disrespectfully on my feet) under the chair. I forced a smile, but the effort must have produced a maniacal look because she began examining the folds of her pink and gold sari, no doubt silently incanting that the indisputable dirty whore, slut, tramp sitting in her home vanish. I suspected she might already be planning a purification ritual for the moment I left. I said my own prayers for that to happen soon.

Manya, Ishita's 17-year-old daughter, served us tall glasses of room-temp water with hands lavishly decorated in the ancient art of henna *mehndi*. When she reached me with the last glass on the tray, she chanced a brief smile before hustling back to the kitchen. She'd kept her expression hidden from the others, especially her mother, but her 14-year-old brother Yash, who'd sidled into the room after we arrived, didn't care what his mother thought. He beamed openly at me, probably wondering if the rumors about Western women's sexual appetites were true.

The room crackled with an odd dynamic that made me think Ahana didn't like her brother and sister-in-law any more than I did. Maybe she sensed their disapproval of me, whom she proudly showed off. Either way, it struck me that she rushed through her obligations as she presented Sai with an ostentatiously large and lavishly spangled rakhi the size of an orange. She fastened it expertly to his considerable wrist before pressing her fingertips into a delicate ceramic pot she extracted from her purse and smudged a red *tilak* onto his forehead. She ceremoniously hand-fed him a gooey sweet, sticky with honey and dusted in crushed bright green pistachios, before repeating the ritual with Yash. I hoped Angel and Queenie would not take part. When they didn't, I felt gleeful, until it occurred to me that maybe they simply weren't old enough yet.

Manya reemerged from the kitchen with bowls of *gulab jamun*, a crispy dumpling swimming in syrup, and for once I was grateful for the speed at which most Indians I knew ate. After the second round of water appeared, Ahana stood and announced we must go. I felt Ishita's scorching scowl on my back as I stepped out of her dreary home and into the sunlight.

24

A Woman's Place

"Locked!" Rushil said, sounding puzzled and looking around outside Ahana's younger brother's home.

"Locked?" Ahana echoed, as we stood in front of the iron gate that covered the solid front door.

I noted Ahana's use of English became more frequent the longer we were together. Rushil giggled and shuffled his feet while holding up the heavy padlock that dangled from the gate as evidence. It looked like something from the Dark Ages or from a Vincent Price movie. Ahana squeezed her hands and squinted wanly at me as Rushil gave the lock another hopeless yank.

"Listen," Rushil said. "Someone inside."

We hushed and leaned toward the door, hearing a cough and shambling feet before the heavy wood door creaked slowly open. Kiara, Ahana's sister-in-law, greeted us dejectedly. She wasn't dressed in splendor like Ahana but wore a dishwater drab salwar kameez that looked as if it was used to scrub the floor and spoke lifelessly to Rushil.

"She says Mother has gone to the market with Kiara's daughter. Yug is at his club."

It mystified me how Ahana's mother could mistakenly lock her daughter-in-law in the house when she went to the market, and I asked Rushil about it.

"No mistake," he said, another giggle eking out. "Mother's eyes on everyone."

I wasn't sure what he meant but guessed Mother might be the suspicious and controlling type. Rushil seemed nervous, but I couldn't tell if it was because of the treatment of his sister-in-law or that I witnessed it.

While Rushil and Ahana talked with Kiara through the iron bars, Angel and Queenie teetered on one leg like storks in shiny dresses and I slumped my achey back against the house. After about ten minutes, Mother marched up the walk with four-year-old Pari prancing at her side. Ahana and Rushil greeted the matriarch with bows, hugs, and smiles. She returned their hellos reservedly without acknowledging me—even though her radar was on high alert—and fished an iron key, the length of a child's arm, from her sari's waistband and unlocked the gate.

Ahana ushered us into a dark sitting room studded with glossy framed posters of Krishna and Shiva. The gods scrutinized me peevishly in the cold, impersonal, and unloved room's harsh fluorescent lights. The only spark of life emanated from Pari, who outshined her cousins in spunkiness. She twirled over to me, cocked her head appraisingly, and tossed me a cat-that-swallowed-the-canary grin, before bouncing off to join Angel and Queenie in another room.

Ahana, Rushil, Mother, and I settled onto sofas and chairs, and, just like at Sai's house, the three of them talked and ignored me. I detected no mention of me at first. Mother was so happy to see her only daughter, and it was easy to see where Ahana's exuberance came from, but that's where the resemblance stopped. Mother threw her head back and brayed like a donkey, exposing a toothless pink maw. Her belly protruded pregnantly under the pleats of her sari but the rest of her wizened body disappeared into the sari's folds. Her voice tinkled melodically when speaking to anyone other than her daughter-in-law Kiara, then the words were barbed wire. I wondered why she hated her since she'd no doubt chosen her as Yug's bride. Had Mother been treated badly by her mother-in-law and was acting out a legacy? I found myself hoping Ahana never had a son; that Queenie and Angel would be her only children, fearing if she did bear a son she'd turn into her mother.

Rushil and Ahana had laughed off the fact that Kiara was locked in the house like chattel when we arrived saying, "India," and shrugging as if to mean, "What can we do?"

I knew it was part of the heinous treatment some Indian women suffered. The newspapers' reports of "kitchen fires" killing young brides or acid being thrown into the faces of women who scorned men's affections or been raped on buses in broad daylight sickened and enraged me. Faulty gas cylinders didn't cause all "kitchen fires," rather it could be a euphemism for murder committed by a greedy groom's family to get rid of a bride whose family ran out of dowry money. Sometimes the reports implicated the mothers-in-law as starting the fires. I never understood how women could do such a thing to each other.

Being aware of oppression and facing it as a guest in someone's home was a situation I wasn't prepared for. Over the years, I played a game of "what if," plugging in various scenarios and how I'd react, but it had never occurred to me to consider what I'd do if I encountered a woman enslaved in her own home. I responded to the harsh treatment of Kiara by pathetically crossing my arms in disapproval. My heart knew it wasn't enough. My head knew there was little else I could do.

Kiara stayed in the kitchen until Mother ordered her to serve refreshments, and then her eyes remained averted as she placed glasses of water and bowls of snacks on the too-low coffee table. Her tan salwar kameez hung loose on her raw-boned body and her lackluster hair was pulled into a hapless bun. Her sadness permeated the room and Rushil quietly explained she'd been crying because Mother would not allow her to visit her brother until she served us lunch and cleaned up. That wouldn't happen until after Yug returned from his club and Ahana performed her rituals and presented him with his rakhi.

Ahana had left the living room sometime earlier, leaving me to sit with Rushil and Mother in silence. The living room air was stuffy, and I thought about stepping outside, but couldn't figure out how to leave the room without seeming rude, and my Midwestern upbringing scorned rudeness.

As the girls skipped into the room, Mother turned her curiosity on me, quizzing Rushil in a tone used for cajoling kittens into a gunny sack before dropping them into a lake.

"I told her I know you many years. That we go to college together," Rushil confided between Mother's questions. "If I not tell her this, she not want you in her home. To Mother, truth sounds very bad."

From the look in Mother's bird-of-prey eyes he hadn't fooled her, as they flashed, "I've-got-your-number girlie."

"She doesn't like me," I said to Rushil while smiling at Mother. "Look at her face."

"Mother be always looking like this," Rushil sniggered. "Mother watches."

I closed my eyes waiting for brother number two to come home and listened to Kiara clattering in the kitchen. I'd not eaten all day and was sinking into one of the sofa's many crevices when Angel came and took my hand, leading me to the bedroom where Ahana and Queenie lay on a bed. Ahana patted a spot next to her, and I gratefully climbed in as Angel and Queenie flanked me. Pari galloped into the room demanding to join us, but we were already two too many and Ahana sent her to join Rushil, whom she'd heard retreat to the screened porch after I abandoned him with Mother. Pari stomped away at the rebuff. I rolled onto my side and fell asleep in the cloying heat, waking sometime later as Ahana gently rocked my shoulder and whispered, "Lunch, Coney."

Yug had returned from his club bringing a mean energy with him. Slouched in an armchair, sporting a tidal wave of black hair and a thorny mustache, he looked like a gangster. His pocked face and baritone voice slammed across the room and shook my insides. Even his children, Pari and her baby brother, Zayan, navigated away from him, avoiding his aura as if it stung them.

"Whiskey," Yug shouted at Kiara in the kitchen, then reached over and slapped Rushil on the back; he flinched and gulped down a giggle.

The men had eaten by the time Ahana woke me and were drinking Jack Daniels' Black Label whiskey with warm Thumb's Up cola. I joined the women and children at the dining table. Kiara scurried back and forth with fresh fat *puris* and steaming bowls of *subzi*. She wouldn't be allowed to eat until we had our fill, and then she'd eat alone in the kitchen.

"Same. Same. Every Raksha Bandhan," Ahana said, as she pointed to each heaping dish of food Kiara plunked on the table:

bhindis, aloo, pakoras, dhal, sweet milk. Ahana looked pleased as she told me, and I understood her to mean that the meal was traditional, like a Thanksgiving feast. Mother and Ahana picked at their portions, but Mother insisted I put more food onto my already heaping plate as she ordered Kiara to refill the emptied bowls. If it were anyone but Mother piling up my plate, I'd have thought she was being hospitable, but I didn't think of Mother as nice. She either wanted to make me sick or force poor Kiara to work harder. Probably both.

"Koonneee, come," Yug called from the other room, "Have whiskey."

I don't drink whiskey. I got drunk on it when I was sixteen years old and since then the smell and sight of it replayed revolting memories. But the command offered an escape from Mother and her attempt to founder me like a horse, so I excused myself and settled into a chair as far from Yug as possible. Curious about the source of the liquor, I ask him where he got his alcohol since Gujarat was a dry state.

"Yes, it is dry, but this is India," he said. "We have everything if you know the right people."

I'd heard that line before and didn't doubt it. Why would India work differently than the rest of the world?

"I know the right people," he continued, taking a leisurely swig from a cheap tumbler. "At my club, there are many important men."

A silly grin crept onto Rushil's face and he chuckled for no reason. He looked wobbly in the chair too. He told me the day before that he didn't drink alcohol because it was "wrong." He must have read my thoughts because he slurred apologetically, "I only drink on special occasions."

"That is true," Yug said, putting his bear-like paw on his small brother-in-law's shoulder with such force Rushil nearly toppled over. "Do you know why?" he continued. "Because he is a very good man."

I thought so, but wondered what Yug was suggesting.

"So good that people give him money! Give him money because he is good, and," he paused, allowing anticipation to climax, "so he will give them land."

Across the room, Ahana, Mother, and the children had finished eating and vanished, leaving me alone with the men. Rushil hadn't drunk so much liquor that his brother-in-law's implication escaped him. He shook his head, the alcohol sloshing his features as he struggled to deny Yug's accusation. I didn't like Yug suggesting Rushil took bribes in his position as a government officer. It might be a way of business in India, but I didn't want to hear these things about Rushil. I wanted to keep my belief that he was an honest, hard-working man who cared for his family, encouraged his wife's independence, and treated her as his equal partner, not Yug's alternate version of him as a corrupt official.

"What can he do?" Yug said, waving his glass about, letting his words hang in the air like the blade of a guillotine. "The peoples force money on him. He does not keep it. No, not a single *paise*. He gives it all to the temples and poor peoples."

First Rushil was a thief and now an Indian Robin Hood? I didn't want to hear that either. I just wanted to think of him as a decent guy. I was considering how I could respond when Yug's son Zayan blundered into the room, reeled along by his tubby belly. He wore a T-shirt but no pants. A band of red threads was tied around his belly to ward off evil spirits, and his eyes were ringed in kajal—to ugly him up so demons wouldn't steal him. He stopped and his enormous head rotated my direction, resting his large eyes on me before taking a few stumbling steps. Grateful he appeared and disrupted the conversation, I watched Yug coax Zayan to him, but the child stood blinking and swaying hesitantly, in a manner that made me wonder if there was something mentally wrong with him.

"His big head is blessing. Sign of great intelligence," Rushil said, stifling a snicker behind three fingers.

I wanted to leave. Be done with Raksha Bandhan and the whole family affair. It was after 5 p.m. and both the day and I were drained. Plus, it was a long ride back to Bhuj. Ever attuned, Ahana came into the living room and announced we were leaving. I hadn't seen her secure Yug's blessing with a rakhi but figured she did it before waking me for lunch.

"Thirty minutes," Rushil said, an act of defiance for Yug's benefit. His head drooped drunkenly to one side and Ahana, seeing he was on the verge of passing out, said, "Come, Coney. Sleep."

On the way to the bedroom, I passed Kiara in the corridor dressed in a stiff, blue synthetic sari, towing Pari in a frilly frock and carrying pant-less Zayan, on her way to her brother's home for her Raksha Bandhan celebration. I wanted to say something to her, to apologize and acknowledge the wrongs I thought she endured, but she didn't look at me. That struck me as wrong. I should have been the one unable to meet her eyes.

25

Over the Edge

The stinging sensation on my palm and the pinking of the man's mahogany cheek told me I'd slapped him. I had no memory of it. I remembered the boys taunting me and the gentle old man trying to protect me. I remembered my anger at their victimization of the old man and me. I remembered the man on the scooter shielding the boys from me. I remembered the throng of male onlookers pressing in around us: me, the old man, and the man on the scooter. I remembered the silence in that vortex of men. I remembered the utter aloneness I felt in the crowd. I remembered the fleeting inkling: was this what insanity was like—to lose touch with the self you thought you knew, to drift so far from the rail of your reality that you become something unrecognizable?

काली

Forty-two days had elapsed since I'd left New Delhi, and eleven since I'd left Ahana and Rushil in Bhuj. I visited their small family several times after Raksha Bandhan before heading into the Rann of Kutchch to explore the famous salt marsh where salmon-pink flamingos wintered, but it was early August, and none strutted on spindly legs.

I'd arrived in Ahemdabad—described in my guidebook as "a European oasis"—in need of India to be a bit less Indian. I'd sought similar refuge a few days earlier in Nagoa Beach in Diu, a tiny ex-Portuguese colony on the Arabian Sea in southern Gujarat. I went there in hopes of meeting other travelers, but instead spent two nights in a grimy room next to a stinky communal squat toilet. During my stay, ants had nested in my helmet's honeycomb foam padding as it hung on the wall, a discovery I didn't make until I put it on the morning I left the hotel. They crawled out of the foam and down into my ears, pinching and biting me to the brink of madness as I rode, causing me to wildly jerk Kali to the side of the road and pull the helmet from my head. In a crazed frenzy, I slapped and pawed at my head, killing all the ants I could. I didn't dare ride without a helmet in India, so I suffered the ants for days. The battle with ants, my failure to do something for Kiara, the groping hijras, the crazy old man who fired fake bullets at me, the isolation and fatigue from the road, and the constant violation of my space and privacy by strangers left me feeling like a frayed wire: unprotected and unpredictable.

Taking a back road to Ahemdabad, I arrived shortly before sunset and checked into a hotel. Leaving Kali in the hotel's lot, I set out in search of a Continental-style cafe but rather than discovering a vibrant eatery, I found myself on empty sidewalks surrounded by shuttered businesses looking up at a marquee proclaiming, "PRINCESS DIANA DEAD." I didn't believe it. Figured it was a joke or some crazy misinformation. But I couldn't get her off my mind as I wandered away. I wasn't an ardent admirer of Lady Di but she brought goodness to the world and the thought of her being gone made me lonelier.

The streets led me to the Sabarmati River, where lovers promenaded hand-in-hand in the twilight across Nehru Bridge, the gold-trimmed pallus of the ends of the women's saris fluttered like iridescent sails on high seas. They'd come out to "meet the breeze," but it reeked of the briny river-water peppered with rotting fish. I sat on a bench, closed my eyes, and soaked up the evening's ambiance as images of Princess Diana imbued my mind. The sound of slapping bare feet disturbed my peace, and a reedy voice said, "Namaste." Opening my eyes, I found two smirking boys in scruffy blue shorts with their scrawny arms thrust at me like little lances.

"Shake," said the taller of the two. They looked to be about ten years old and their wide grins split their umber faces, showing straight rows of big, white, piano-key teeth. Their eagerness to shake the hand of a *firang*, a foreigner, was cute, and as I pumped their frail arms up and down, their grins grew bigger and bigger with each thrust. When I stopped, they cried for more and so I obliged. I refused their third command. They insisted, moving closer until their hard, little feet touched the tips of my boots.

"Shake," repeated the smallest boy, whose cuteness became demonic.

"No more," I said, and looked out over the water. I hoped the gesture would shoo them away, but they remained rooted in front of me, their arms aimed, cocked, and ready.

I rose and began walking away, the boys falling in step behind me shouting, "Shake." I sped up, taking long strides and letting my hands swing at my sides. As my right arm arced back, one of the boys slapped my hand. I spun around, and they skittered away laughing and ribbing each other with their pointy elbows. I scowled and took a few quick steps in their direction to scare them. They scurried off and I turned away, thinking that was the end of it.

A stooped old man drifted toward me through the ebb and flow of lovers. His face was like a walnut, dark and crevassed, that he held high like a carving on a ship's prow. He had a dignified air even though he was unshaven, and his clothes were abused and worn. Mesmerized by the rhythm of his shuffling, lopsided gait as he threaded through the throngs, I didn't realize the boys had returned until they flew past me, encircling the old man and me. They shoved the old man at me. He stumbled, his mouth opened with surprise, and I reached to catch him. He clung to me, struggling to straighten himself as the boys bolted into the crowd shrieking in satisfaction. The words "little fuckers" sprang into my mind and possibly out of my mouth as I steadied the old man. He bowed and pressed his hands apologetically together, prayer-like as if it were his fault.

The boys returned, prancing around and kicking rocks at us with their stony feet. I'd been the target of menacing kids before, in both India and the Middle East, and knew they were not harmless simply because they were children. Especially in numbers. These two jittered around us slapping at our arms and legs with their sharp, ragged nails. The old man reached for our taunters but only caught air. I bellowed, "Go Away" and lunged at them, catching one's shirttail. He broke away and ducked behind a man sitting on a scooter. The second boy joined him, and together they hid behind the man. He didn't appear to notice them, but the old man and I saw their pinched, hateful faces, their evil grins peeking between the arms and legs of their protector. The old man and I yelled at the boys, attempting to snatch them from their bodyguard, but they hunkered lower, their grins igniting an unholy rage in me.

I smelled the sickly coconut oil in their guardian's hair, saw his red-stained teeth from chewing betel. He seemed oblivious to what was going on and stared past us as he inhaled long, leisurely drags on a stubby cigarette. The old man and I fulminated and gesticulated wildly. I wanted to get my hands on the boys, to march them down to the traffic cop on the corner. I wanted to teach them a lesson, to let them know it wasn't okay to torment people. I wanted them to feel the consequences of their behavior. Boys like this grew into men like Yug, and the memory of Kiara snuffling around dejected and abused still angered me. I no longer saw the two boys as having a lark; instead, they represented every male-perpetrated wrong I'd ever encountered.

The old man finally got the scooter guy's attention and said something to him, but the guy shook his head no. I wondered if he was their father, uncle, or simply the biggest man on the street the kids could take refuge with? The old man stopped talking to the man on the scooter and stepped back. Maybe he'd said all he had to say, or maybe he knew when to let something go and walk away. But I didn't. I clung to my righteousness.

I saw the police officer standing in the intersection half a block away, and my hands twitched to grab one of the boys. It didn't matter which one, either would do. Insisting he give me one of the boys to take to the police, I shouted at the man protecting them until he did. I gripped the back of the boy's frail shirt fabric in my fist and tugged him toward the officer. My desire for retribution was so intense that if the boy made a sound, I didn't hear him.

The police officer was still a long way off when a hot grip clamped my wrist and nails dug into my flesh. The man from the scooter pried at my fingers clutching the boy's shirt. He'd changed his mind, but I wouldn't release my prize and tightened my grasp. He wrested my fingers loose one-by-one until the boy escaped. That's when I slapped the man; except, I don't remember doing that. All I recall is the sting on my hand and the repugnance in his black eyes.

Within seconds, a crowd of men crushed us—their bleary-faces loomed at me from all angles. The old man squeezed through the battalion and tugged his earlobes; a sign Indians use to beg forgiveness. But what needed forgiving? Was he imploring me for forgiveness, or for me to forgive? Who deserved such mercy?

His sad eyes floated in his mouse-like face as he yanked on his pendulous earlobes. Dark, bristly faces bobbed around us, straining to glimpse what was going on. Had I been in control of myself, had I a heart, I'd have stopped and walked away. Instead, I spun toward the man I'd slapped, saw my own rancor reflected in his eyes, and knew it would end badly.

The old man pressed his hands together and raised trembling arms high overhead pleading in English, "Forgive, madam. Forgive." But I couldn't. Something insidious had a stranglehold on me. I was a warrior, Kali, hell-bent on someone paying.

"Leave it, madam," shouted the agitated men. "Leave it."

The old man wedged between the man and me again, repeating, "Good man. Bad boy. Okay?" His pleading distracted me as the crowd swallowed the man.

"Leave it," said two men, pushing to the front of the group as I caught sight of the man working his way out of the crowd. I struggled after him. The pack squeezed tighter chanting, "Leave it. Leave it. Leave it. Leave it." An opening in the herd appeared and I saw the man hop onto the bridge's wall. He turned and looked sublimely at me, then disappeared. I knifed my way to the spot and peered over the edge into a velvety black chasm. A six-foot plummet spanned the bridge to the alleyway below. I flung myself violently over the edge.

Hitting the hard ground, I rose on newfound legs. The man's footfalls echoed as he vanished into the pitch. I plunged after him, headlong into the inky tunnel. Fragments of light filtered in from yellow streetlights. I spotted flashes of his shirt flitting ahead of me. I ran harder, my feet pounding the alley's hard surface, driven by a voice inside demanding, *Get him.*

I was gaining ground when my worn boot snagged on an old root, hurdling me to my hands and knees. Shards of glass bit into the heels of my hands as the hard earth punched the breath from my body. Deflated, I crouched in the deserted alley stunned and shattered by what I'd done—who I'd become—as my breath slowly returned.

In the muggy air, thick with the fetid stench of rotten fruit and old urine, I prayed the earth would swallow me. Prayed the goddesses would pity me enough for this to be a nightmare. But the taste of blood in my mouth from biting my tongue and gouges in the palms of my hands told me it was real. Who was I? How had I arrived at this broken state?

My knee throbbed, and I was grateful to be cradled by darkness. Unable to move, I hugged myself and listened to my thudding heart. I'd wanted someone to pay; someone had. Me.

26

Restitution

Seeking solace far from Ahemdabad, I rose early the next day and followed the signs to Surat, a small town attached to the outskirts of Mumbai like a wart. Its citizens were in the throes of preparing for Ganesh Chaturthi, a festival honoring the god Ganesh, the elephant-headed god who removes obstacles from the paths of believers.

I checked into a newly built motel, redolent with the aroma of fresh paint, parking Kali in the rear. The place felt deserted and I seemed to be the only guest, making me the sole concern of the two fastidious young men in charge. Dressed sharply in creased uniforms, one penned my name and passport details neatly into the hotel ledger, then the other escorted me down a long exterior balcony that fronted the facade to a quiet room at the end. The room was bright, clean, and basic but lacked a lock on the door. I pointed this out to the bellhop, who nodded agreeably and hustled away. I began undressing, to take my first real shower in days, when he burst back into the room saying, "Lock coming, ma…." His eyes bulged at the sight of my naked flesh, clad only in a sport bra, as I scrambled to cover myself.

The roads diminished my appetite and whittled fifteen pounds from my waifish frame. More than my desire for food had vanished, my interest in locating any more of the shakti peetha temples dissipated too. Locating them proved too problematic. The last one I attempted to discover a few days earlier near Chorwad, Gujarat, resulted in an argument between two priests of nearby temples, each claiming his was a shakti peetha.

When I left New Delhi, I thought I needed to find the temples and pieces of Kali to guide and empower me on my journey. But I'd come to understand finding them didn't do that. Being on the road, on my own day after day, was what made me strong and whole. Each day since riding out of New Delhi I'd felt the timid girl I once was grow fainter in me. In her place was a woman—going, doing, being—in the world.

I decided not to look for any more temples but still wanted to reach Kolkata in time for Kali Puja on October 30, remembering Patralekha's words about it being a celebration I needed to see. I had fifty-eight days to ride 3,100 miles, an average of fifty-three miles a day to make it in time.

काली

The hotel offered everything necessary to stay sequestered until I was ready to reemerge into the world: cable television, hot showers, clean sheets, and a staff willing to fetch me food from nearby restaurants. I was stretched out on the bed, holed up and inert for a day watching BBC coverage of Princess Diana's and Mother Teresa's funerals—they'd died within days of each other —when someone rapped on my door shouting, "Madam. Madam. You are wanted."

It was about 9:30 p.m. and no one except the two young men running the place knew I was there. I opened the door and the eager faces of the two grinned back at me.

"What's wrong? Is there a problem with my motorcycle?" I asked.

"Come, come. Outside. Visitors, madam," they said in unison, feverishly beckoning me to follow them.

"Wait," I shouted, as they rushed along the balcony. "What visitors?"

They didn't slow, and when I caught up with them, they pointed to the street below.

"The children!" said the one I presumed to be the manager. "They see madam come motorcycle. Come Kali. They never see madam come motorcycle. Never."

Under a sprawling tree that looked out of place on a busy city street, wiggled dozens of barefoot children against a backdrop of careening traffic. The congregation consisted of mostly girls aged ten or eleven, one or two boys, and a scattering of women and men, all gleefully waving and hollering "Hello. Hello. Hello. Hello. Hello."

"Say something, madam," said the manager. "Children come speak you."

His reverential tone struck me as one used to urge a Queen to address her subjects. But I wasn't someone to admire. Besides, what could I say to children I'd never met? Even if I did find the words, my Hindi wouldn't suffice. Would they understand English?

"Happy see you, madam. Speak," the bellhop piped in.

I looked at the bouncing crowd below, jittering with anticipation, their beatific faces glowing in the vaporous night air. Their yearnings wriggled into my heart, easing some of the sting that lingered from the incident with the man on the bridge. Still, what harm was there in being friendly? They were slum kids looking for joy.

"I have nothing to say," I argued.

"Madam must. Children want you speak."

"Maybe I should go down to them," I heard myself say.

"No, madam," shrieked the clerk. "You must not. They be *jhuggi* children."

I thought of the boys in Ahemdabad and how innocent they'd seemed when they'd first approached me, then I looked at the exuberant children, grinning and flapping their tiny hands, unable to control their excitement as their bare feet stirred up dust clouds.

From a distance, I saw no physical difference between these slum kids and those two boys when I first encountered them. The only thing different was me. I enjoyed kids' company but now stood wary and reserved. I'd played and engaged with thousands of kids from dozens of countries without incident during my travels. Was I going to allow one or two experiences to change me, cause me to give up these happy encounters?

"Stay, madam," the clerk cautioned as if sensing I was about to do something risky.

He was right, it was safer to stay on the balcony, far removed from the life below. But that contradicted my reason for being on the road. I came to break free of my fears.

I moved toward the staircase, drawn by their euphoric faces like the moon pulls the tide.

Both the manager and bellhop scampered after me, calling, "Wait, madam. Wait." As I neared the children, their numbers seemed to swell, and I wondered if I'd miscalculated the scenario.

The girls hopped about, gushing with anticipation as I neared them, asking, "What name? Where from?"

A folding chair mysteriously appeared; I was ushered to it by two women and encouraged to sit. They instructed the children to gather and settle at my feet, making me feel like a kindergarten or Sunday school teacher about to deliver a message. The kids squirmed into place, notching themselves together like pieces of a puzzle, and introduced themselves. Thumping their chests each precisely pronouncing their name: Sheetal, Pinky, Jayshri, Anil, Kisal, Anita, Namreta, Ishita, Darmish, Premila, Herentral, Chetna, Janex, Manisha, Priyanka, Darmista, Usa, Sunita, Mandra, Ravindra, and so on.

When it was my turn, I said, *"Mere nam* Connie *hai."*

Their eyes glittered as they tasted my name, its foreignness like sweet, sticky taffy on their tongues as they intoned, Konee, Koonee, Kanee.

I retrieved a pen from my pocket and carefully composed my name in Hindi on the palm of the little girl named Pinky. She stared at it as if being handed a treasure, tracing each letter with her tiny finger, absorbing each mark's sound before proudly pronouncing it Kawnee. She giggled and the crowd laughed. The act unwittingly unleashing a tsunami of requests, as every child thrust his or her hand at me chanting, "Autograph. Autograph."

A woman bustled forward and settled the kids down and formed them into a line for me to sign their little hands. The hotel manager resurfaced armed with a proprietary sense of me and insisted I return to my room, reminding me my dinner was getting cold. Word of my appearance and autograph session had spread and the line of anxious children strung out of sight—speckled with a few adults. I didn't want to leave them. The little ones' enthusiasm and spirit, their eagerness to connect, their desire to exchange some pieces of themselves for a piece of me was healing. It was also draining, and I was grateful for the clerk's overbearing insistence I return to my room as an opportunity to escape. I promised the kids I'd visit them at their homes the next day.

As the clerk escorted me to safety, Pinky grabbed my hand and kissed it, setting off another chain reaction as others tried to do the same, but the clerk shooed them away.

27

The Gang

Pinky and a crew of six or seven girls dressed in an array of salwar-kameez suits, pleated parochial skirts and blouses, and Mickey Mouse T-shirts over trousers, waited for me early the next morning. A couple of little bare-chested boys in shorts were part of the pack but the girls were clearly in charge. As I approached them Pinky took my right hand while the others attached themselves to various parts of me like suckerfish on a whale. Walking in the puddle of children, I feared stepping on their bare feet with my boots. I tried to tell them this, but they only giggled and clutched me tighter.

Pinky pointed at a little boy with a dirty face who she called Kisal, miming what I understood as "silly boy can't take care of himself." Kisal swiveled his face toward me displaying a turned-down mouth, then broke into an impish grin and spit on his hands, rubbing them furiously over his face. The girls twittered and smiled at his futility.

Sheetal, one of the older girls and drowning in a too-big, green salwar-kameez, informed me they were learning English in school. I was glad to hear they were being schooled since education among the poor wasn't a priority, and less so for girls. I wondered why they weren't in school now but knew there were several reasons to explain it, ranging from the teacher didn't show up to my visit beat going to school any day. The educational class difference was distinct. Wealthy Indian kids faced tremendous pressure to perform at the tops of their classes, but these *jhuggi* kids didn't experience the same academic urgency. Many, especially the girls, helped their families earn money until they were married off. Families kept the boys in school as long as economically possible, to improve their ability to attract a wealthier bride.

The children shuttled me along like ants trotting a treat to their homes in a nearby settlement. Squatting along the bank of an open ditch, rife with raw sewage and fecal matter, huddled a collection of homes cobbled together from discarded bricks, slats of wood, and sheets of corrugated iron.

A debate broke out between Pinky and Sheetal as we entered the camp over whose house I'd visit. I promised to go to each of their homes, and their fight shifted to whose home I went to first. Pinky won, and we trooped into a surprisingly cool cave-like dwelling with an earthen living-room floor polished hard and smooth by bare feet. A charpoy occupied one side of the room and a shiny tin trunk the other. The Indian government habitually destroyed such impromptu housing encampments, but this one appeared to have been standing for some time. Its mud walls were whitewashed and displayed colorful posters of gods and goddesses, frameless and ensconced behind thick plastic to protect them. The scent of *nag champa* incense spiced the air and snuffed out the stinky ditchwater. It felt homey and loved inside.

A dozen-plus children crowded into the room, sitting on the floor or leaning against the wall while several women crouched alongside them and in a doorframe that led to a cooking area.

Pinky escorted me to the charpoy, as if leading an elderly queen, and scooted in next to me, snuggling close. A woman in a coffee-colored floral salwar kameez named Urmila sat on the other side of me. She spoke some English and acted as my interpreter for the others. She was the mother of three of the children, but I couldn't figure out which ones.

Upon my arrival, one of the women had folded some rupees into Kisal's palm and sent him out to fetch a Pepsi which she presented to me. I didn't want it, knowing it would be warm and sting my throat, but their generosity touched me. They didn't have money to spare, and the extravagance of a Pepsi instead of the knockoff Thumbs Up deepened the gesture. I sipped obligingly as the women whispered to each other about me. They had questions.

"Do you have children?" asked Urmila, their spokesperson.

I considered lying to them, saying I had sons who were married to beautiful wives. That would make them happy. I'd fabricated other truths about my life while traveling, like the cheap wedding band. I didn't want to lie to these women, yet I didn't want to repeat the experience I had with Ahana either and reinforce preconceived cultural ideas.

Pinky saved me by tugging at my hand and towing me to see their Ganesh shrines out back in a little courtyard between the dwellings. Surrounded by a smattering of kids was a foot-tall Ganesh perched on a pedestal and draped in red tinsel. One leg was folded under his round body and he benevolently raised his right hand in *mundra,* symbolizing "fear not," while the other cradled lotus flowers. The ground around him swelled with offerings of conch shells, hairy coconuts, strings of jasmine. A smoldering incense smoked swirls around the elephant god. I oohed to their delight as the jarring sounds of sitars, flutes, and tablas began pounding Bollywood tunes from a radio inside.

Jhuggis weren't legal structures and therefore not wired with electricity, but people found ways to tap into it anyway. Pinky hauled me back inside. Grabbing Sheetal's hands, they swiveled their hips and shoulders, playfully mimicking the film stars they loved. Urmila and the other mothers clapped, their jingling bangles adding subtle notes to the songs, while Kisal and another little boy stomped and bobbed their heads, googling their eyes as love-sick movie stars did on the big screen. I nursed my warm soda while everyone gyrated around me.

Pinky and Sheetal noticed my absence and grabbed my arms, insisting I join them—eager to see how my Western moves matched their Eastern sways. It wasn't a contest. Despite my mom's fantasy of me becoming a ballerina, I don't like being on display and am awkward, clunky, and rhythmless when it comes to dancing. My moves brought pitches of laughter from everyone. The girls tried to teach me some steps. They shook their ankles and stamped their pretty bare feet, the tinkle of their bracelets lilting in the air as they clapped their hands. It was hopeless.

When they finally let me sit down, I thought the party was over, but that wouldn't happen for hours. After dancing and drinking a Pepsi at Pinky's house, we hoofed over to Sheetal's home for a repeat performance, then Ishita's, Jayshri's, and Mandra's. My bloated belly ached from the copious bottles of carbonation I obligingly drank between dances. They eventually released me, but only after I promised to visit again.

Later that night, as I watched the *X-Files* and ate chow mein, a chorus of little voices called from the street below, Kawnee, Konee, Koonee, Kanee....

28

Love/Hate

During the miles to Goa, a tourist-destination state on the coast of the Arabian Sea, I rode in and out of pockets of sunshine and light rain all day. I'd stayed in Surat for several days, venturing into Mumbai to explore the markets and chat with other travelers in the Leopold Cafe, famous for attracting Westerners and a site Islamic terrorists bombed in 2008. I'd met a Swedish guy there who was riding a Bullet across India too. He considered himself an expert on everything and pontificated negatively on Nanna. Talking to him made me wonder why I'd ever longed for the company of other Westerners, and left for Goa the next day, overnighting at a four-star hotel in Chiplun.

A rainbow gave way to twilight as I crested a summit on the outskirts of the tourist mecca. Goa, a former Portuguese port, didn't officially secede to become part of India until 1987. The highway led me through a string of beach towns, each promising relaxation and fun. I followed the rainbow, the first I'd ever seen in India and a good omen, to Calungut. By the time I arrived, night had fallen and the village, void of streetlights, was saturated in blackness punctuated by the occasional autorickshaws' headlights. Most drivers didn't use them, to save battery power. Kali's horn had stopped working and now her headlamp chose that moment to blink out. Using the lights of other vehicles when possible, I navigated around amorphous figures. After a few near misses, involving scrawny dogs and bossy chickens, I located a beachfront, bare-bones hotel and called it a night.

I woke late the next morning and wandered over to an Italian cafe I'd spotted the night before. September was off-season in Goa, so I wasn't sure what I'd find, but the cafe's thatched roof, red and white checkered tablecloths fluttering in the ocean breeze, and wine-bottles caked in candle wax charmed me. I hoped it served breakfast or at least offered coffee and toast as I settled into the plastic chair at a table in the sun. An Indian man in his early thirties dressed in a faded Hard Rock Cafe T-shirt and well-worn jeans ambled over.

"What would you like? Eggs? Toast?" he said, a lilting rhythm in his English words.

I ordered scrambled eggs, buttered toast, and coffee and he headed for the kitchen as I gazed at the sea, watching a line of silver waves burst as they hit the shore. The beach and most of the surrounding restaurants were deserted and lonely looking, even though it was mid-morning, and I wished I'd brought a book to read.

"Your meal will be a few minutes still," said the waiter. "I've sent my guy to buy some bread. If you want jam, I can send someone for that too."

The service impressed me, especially after the treatment I got at a four-star resort in Chiplun. It promised a Western-style buffet and I'd imagined it would be like the champagne brunches in New Delhi, minus the champagne. Instead, it served too-spicy dhal swimming in ghee and a few stale chapattis. When I complained, the waiter delivered a bleak expression and strolled off.

"No. That's okay," I said.

"My name's Samar. Mind if I sit with you?"

I considered him more closely: tall and slightly pudgy, with a black goatee and warm caramel eyes. I guardedly nodded. He said he owned the cafe but had grown up in Hong Kong with his Anglo-Indian Christian mother and Italian stepfather. He'd returned to India three years ago after reuniting with his father to start a business. He didn't tack "madam" to the end of every sentence and lacked the predatory look of some men. We talked about changing markets and business opportunities in a nation of a billion people. Our easy conversation, the first real one I'd had in months, allowed me to relax. Starved for human companionship, I found myself wondering what it would be like to kiss him? To lean into his chest? To feel his arms encircle me?

The day stretched into afternoon, and I barely registered the sun arching overhead until he mentioned dinner.

"I have to talk to the chef about tonight's menu and organize the supplies," Samar said, "but why don't you join me for drinks and dinner? About sunset?"

The idea of a date made me tingly. I hadn't had a date since Amir and I broke up shortly before I left New Delhi. Samar's invitation made me realize how much I missed romance. I'd planned and packed for every conceivable scenario I might encounter on the road, except a date. I had nothing nice to wear. Even my best clothes were faded and frayed from the constant wearing and hand scrubbing. But there was a pouch of makeup stowed at the bottom of my saddlebags. At the time I packed it, it seemed silly. Now I was grateful, but wondered what weeks in oppressive heat did to purple eyeshadow?

29

Squiring Knight

I left the cafe to replace the bulb in Kali's headlight and get her oil changed—the first work Kali required in my two months on the road. This surprised me, given how Nanna drove the point of all the breakdowns likely to occur.

Afterward, I returned to my shabby hotel to shower, carefully applying plum eyeshadow to my lids and pinking my cheeks with blush. Since swinging my leg over Kali that first time, I hadn't felt feminine. I hadn't felt masculine either, just not womanly. Astride her, a sensation of power rippled in me. I felt in control, decisive, and clear headed. I didn't doubt myself. The impression had always remained even after I dismounted, but now it was gone. Strolling to the cafe giddy with the possibility of romance, I felt desirable and vulnerable as if walking a high wire without a net.

The dining room was empty and I didn't see Samar, so I sat alone on the terrace and ordered a *nimbu pani*, as a fierce sun sizzled into the Arabian sea, sparking the sky in pastels. My lemonade arrived as Samar sauntered over.

"We won't be eating here tonight," he said. "My father wants to attend a restaurant's opening. We will ride with my father and his girlfriend."

I didn't like the idea of my date with Samar becoming a double date with his father and his girlfriend. I'd imagined a quiet dinner for two in the corner of the cafe, the ocean's cool breeze urging us to nuzzle close as we flirted, the way characters did in the romance novels I'd read as a teenager. Hackneyed and formulaic yes, but it appealed to my hungry heart. I wasn't aware of my craving for human connection until an opportunity for romance occurred. The chance to feel "special and desired" replaced the normal "freak and outlier" for the first time since leaving New Delhi. I wanted to belong again.

Since we wouldn't be dining alone, I hoped Samar would join me for a drink. Instead, he hovered over me and said, "My father is waiting."

I got up, my lemonade untouched, and followed him to the car where he held the door open for me as I climbed into the backseat and he joined me. His father, Harish, and his twenty-year-old Korean girlfriend, Princess, awaited in the front. Harish's graying hair and beard matched his steel-rimmed glasses, complimenting his slate trousers and crisp white shirt and contrasting Samar's faded jeans, Rolling Stones T-shirt, and flip-flops. Princess wore a green silk dress that enhanced her honey-brown skin and her ebony hair was knotted in a chignon. I'd done all I could to pretty myself up, but next to Princess I looked and felt like a vagabond in my tatty, road-weary clothes and scraggly hair.

Sitting close to Samar, I inhaled his clean scent our arms and thighs lightly touched, while Harish prattled on about the wealth he'd accumulated as Princess sat as silent as a Kewpie doll. I wondered if she understood any English.

I thought Samar owned the cafe, but Harish's keenness to check out the competition, see what the new owner had going on, made me wonder if he wasn't the real owner.

Food, sand, and surf were Goa's central attractions and its many eateries catered to Western tastes but served poor imitations of Continental dishes. From a distance, many of the restaurants were alluring in the glimmer of fairy lights looping through rafters and trailing along the walls, but up close they could be shabby. This restaurant proved to be the exception, and we arrived at a cozy alfresco place with yellow paper lanterns swaying in the warm tropical breeze. Saffron, teal, and ruby tablecloths were crowned with dancing candlelight and bouquets of yellow jasmine.

"Sunil, my boy," Harish said to the young proprietor as he hurried over to greet us. "You have done an amazing job,' he said, slapping him on the shoulder with a thundering force.

"Thank you, sir," Sunil said, wincing.

"Wasn't that a clever idea I gave you about the lights? Of course it was, they look smashing," Harish said. Looking at Sunil over the tops of his glasses, he added, "How is the food? Good we hope. We don't want to get sick."

"No, sir. It is exceptional. All fresh," stammered Sunil, unnerved by the suggestion.

I felt bad for Sunil and glanced at Samar, but he eyed the restaurant appraisingly, searching for an idea or two to steal.

"You stupid boy, why haven't you said hello to these people," Harish said, waving his hand at Samar and me, but not Princess. She wavered insignificantly in his shadow like the frail flames of the candles. I envied the possibility that Princess didn't understand a word Harish said until Samar, sensing my thoughts, whispered, "Next season my father will have a new girlfriend. He always does."

"Oh, sorry, sir. Yes, Hello. How are you?" Sunil said, while keeping a nervous eye on Harish.

We smiled and complimented the restaurant's glamour. Princess blinked.

We'd barely been seated when Harish began complaining loudly that our drinks were taking too long. It didn't matter that we'd only ordered them seconds earlier, Harish's plan to torpedo the competition was painfully obvious.

"Sorry, sir. They are coming, sir," Sunil said. "Just one minute, sir. I will tend to them personally."

He returned quicker than I would have, saying the drinks were on their way.

"You're a stupid boy. Why are you acting like a child?" Harish hissed. Sunil took the abuse because Harish was an elder, but the young restauranteur's face flexed in vexation and mortification.

To loosen the noose around his neck, Sunil said, "Sir, did you see my mother and sister sitting behind you?"

At the table snuggled next to the column corpulent with jasmin sat two women dressed in glittery saris wearing unreadable expressions as if they hadn't heard a word Harish said to Sunil.

"Oh! Hello. How are you?" Harish said, turning to face them and dishing up an oozy smile. He swiveled back around before they responded, resuming his impeachments of Sunil. "Why didn't you tell us they were here?"

"Sorry, sir. Let me go see about your drinks."

Harish turned back to the ladies and chatted charmingly with them, oblivious to their icy smiles and barely civil nods. Harish's world consisted of only Harish. Samar leaned over and whispered, "Don't take my father seriously. He just likes to have fun." Sure, I thought, like the Romans and their lions with the Christians.

A platter of hors d'oeuvres arrived—sizzling golden-fried coconut shrimp, triangles of sesame-coated toasted paneer, crisp puffs of spicy potato samosas—carried by a thin waiter trailing behind an anxious-looking Sunil. Harish tentatively picked up a shrimp to examine before nibbling it with dread and begrudgingly conceding it was tasty. Ravenous for a piece of shrimp, I considered reaching for one, but both Samar and Princess seemed to be waiting for Harish's consent. He tried the paneer next, spitting it out and declaring it "full of grease." A horrified Sunil ordered the offending food be whisked away, apologies spilling out of him as the skinny waiter hustled the platter away, and with it my hope of anything to eat.

Once Harish succeeded in reducing Sunil to a worthless, stupid, inconsequential nobody with no business running a restaurant, he stood, clapped his hands, and barked, "Chalo," dictating our departure.

Harish filled the ride back to Samar's cafe with reruns of his previous show about his success and I prayed he and Princess would leave Samar and me to dine alone. Instead, Samar served the four of us a delicate angel-hair pasta drizzled with an exquisitely rich lobster bisque while Harish complained the pasta was gummy and the bisque scorched. Princess remained mute and I barely spoke, fearing Harish's wrath if I drew attention to myself.

When Princess and Harish finally left, Samar and I went out on the veranda. He ordered us coffee and dessert: a medley of fresh fruit capped with fresh whipped cream. The salty ocean breeze soothed some of the night's earlier horrors, as I thought about what Samar and I might do after dessert. Perhaps an intimate walk on the deserted beach.

"Do you want to go to a club?" he asked. "Maybe dance?"

The question surprised me. I didn't think of India as having club scenes, probably because I'm not the clubbing type. I was hoping for passion and deflected the suggestion by saying, 'I didn't think there was much going on in the offseason.'

"Goa's got a raging nightlife, with raves lasting till dawn," he said. "Toni's will be packed tonight."

It sounded awful. I longed to sit on the beach enveloped in darkness and cuddled in Samar's strong arms, his goatee nuzzling my skin as his soft lips sought mine.

"We could take a blanket out onto the beach," I said. "Enjoy the ocean breeze and talk?"

"We can do that after the club," he said. "You've got to experience Goa's nightlife."

30

Creatures of the Night

Toni's turned out to be a house at the end of a rutted-out road. Bartenders and waiters bobbed between tall tables made from large, wooden spools scattered across a patio for patrons to perch around. Even with the house's windows bricked over, disco tunes pulsed through the mortar. As Samar and I stood by the bar waiting for a table to open, I surveyed the crowd. A few foreigners who looked as if they'd arrived in the sixties and forgot to go home milled about in a crowd of Indians dressed in designer-knockoffs. Among the oddly simpatico group, I spotted a voluptuous, long-legged blond in a tight gold and black lamé bodysuit stretched over tawny skin, sitting alone and sipping a drink. Her Rapunzel-like hair framed her impeccably made-up face before spilling down her back and curling at her waist. A sweep of sable lashes hovered over cobalt blue eyes and her lips and nails were lacquered red. I stared as she crossed one slender leg over the other, letting her stiletto dangle artfully from her painted toes. I never saw anyone like her outside of a glossy magazine, and her presence made me feel even dowdier.

Samar caught me looking and said, "That's a man you know."

"Of course, it's a man," I said, thinking he meant the guy she leaned over to talk to at a nearby table.

"No, I mean the one in the fishnet bodysuit. She's a man."

My eyes trailed over her, searching for tell-tale maleness and discovered abnormally large feet, big knuckles, and a sharp Adam's Apple lurking in her otherwise slender neck.

"A man?" I whispered, seeing but not believing.

Samar nodded and looked bored. "She's lived here for years and comes to Toni's all the time."

I couldn't tell if she was an Indian or a foreigner and wondered why this outlier chose to live in India. Looking at her, I thought of a story an Australian woman once told me about a scene she'd witnessed in India that summed up women's position. "I saw four men on the side of the road lifting this really big, heavy rock. Four men," she'd repeated, "lifted it and put it on the head of one woman."

I searched the patio to see if there were other women like her, to see if she had a clan like the hijras. Toni's hummed with characters, but none rivaled her. A fleshy young Scandinavian woman in a baggy black tank top and saggy black pants weaving through the tables tripped and fell. Her top shot up, exposing her large white breast. As she struggled to get up, her feet pinned her pants to the floor so that when she stood they pulled down and bared her bottom. A few people looked and one or two giggled, but most acted as if they'd seen it too many times. Samar tapped my arm. "Let's go inside. That's where the action is."

He took my hand and led me inside, passing four British guys discussing motorcycles they'd rented for a week, and a table of irascible Germans, Dutch and French arguing over racism in Europe. We ducked through a narrow door and into an unlit hallway, the sounds of "Saturday Night Fever" quivered toward us like shockwaves as we stepped into a room painted black with a silver disco ball slowly twirling from the ceiling.

The heat in the airless, windowless space assaulted me and sweat beaded on my upper lip as my pupils dilated to take in the dark scene. On the dance floor, the size of a small guest bedroom, a dozen bodies squirmed, gyrated, and bobbed. Indians sporting designer athletic shoes, Levi jeans, and Izod shirts hip-hopped with foreigners clothed in kurtas, lungis, and saris to the disco tunes the disc jockey spun from a small platform. Men and women of all nationalities quaked and collided with each other, heedless of the culture's norms and taboos as their bodies swayed sexually. A young Indian woman flung her lustrous hair into the face of her tall, blond partner who wrapped his tongue around the strands and panted for more. I glanced at Samar. He looked dreamy in the disco light and I leaned into him, feeling his broad chest against my back, as he snaked an arm around my shoulder and across my chest. It felt heavy and hot and wonderful.

Our hips locked, we swayed slightly to the rhythm as I watched a thin Indian guy zippered in a down jacket with a scarf around his neck, madly fling himself from one end of the room to the other. His arms outstretched to clear the way, he miraculously missed hitting anyone in his flights. Transfixed, I watched as the dancers slowed when the music ended, before they groaned or cheered as the DJ spun another song.

Someone bounced a red laser around the room, drawing circles on women's breasts and men's crotches. After a while, the scene turned stale, and the heat and noise forced me to seek fresh air. I nudged Samar, and we squeezed our way toward the door. The guy in the parka had stripped off his coat, exposing a sweater over a flannel shirt as he continued to relentlessly ping-pong himself across the room.

Outside I heard, "AAARRR, give me WHISKEY," and saw the boozy blond who had tripped and exposed herself earlier, rolling her head back and whipping her tongue in and out of her mouth. She looked like the goddess Kali on a warpath. The crowd had thickened, and I didn't see the woman in the fishnet bodysuit. I wondered if she'd left with someone or alone? In the muggy night air, the whole scene suddenly struck me as unhappy and hopeless. Not so much the Indians who thumbed conventions to enjoy themselves, but the foreigners who reeked of misplaced dreams. Seeing them scared me because in some way I was a bit too much like them. I feared I'd become one of the lost souls if I wasn't careful. It's easy to drift in life, marooning yourself someplace you didn't plan to be only to discover it was too late to do anything about it.

The moonlit ride along treelined lanes on the back of Samar's scooter to his house felt natural. It was only later that I recalled he didn't ask me if I wanted to go there or to my hotel. We both seemed to know that his house was where we wanted to be. An unopened condom lay on the bedside table, given to him earlier by Harish he said, but he didn't make a move to open it, sensing I wasn't ready for that level of intimacy. Instead, he held me, and I felt safe and wanted. I fell asleep in his arms with a sense of belonging in my heart that would not last.

काली

In the week that followed, I checked out of my hotel and moved in with Samar. We lounged by the side of a local five-star hotel's pool. We sat out on the beach at night looking at the stars. He cooked me extravagant lunches and dinners. We used the condom and many more. He told me what and when I should eat. He refused to talk to me at times. He left me sitting alone at his restaurant for hours. He had the waiters tell me, "Sorry, madam, boss is busy." He told me he loved me. He held me. He made me cry. I didn't want to be the kind of woman who was okay with a man who made her cry.

When I left a week later, he refused to get up to see me off or say good-bye. I packed in the dark while he pretended to sleep.

31

Helpful Hands

I walked through the muddy streets of Kanniyakumari—India's most southern tip—headed toward the water's edge where the Gulf of Mannar, Lakshadweep Sea, and Indian Ocean mingle and merge into one, searching for a quiet place to let the road's jars and jangles seep from me. My time with Samar left me hollowed out and sad, and I spent nine, fourteen-hour days putting 729 miles between us.

After buying a coffee in a clay cup from a street vendor, I wandered to the waterfront and sat on a bench, propping my boots up on the sea wall. Tourists milled around a memorial containing Mahatma Gandhi's ashes, and vendors hawked painted souvenir shells. I watched the sun slouch into the three waters, spinning sapphire, mulberry, and tangerine as its last hurrah—unaware the shadow of the 3,000-year-old Kumari Amman Temple I sat in possessed the goddess Kali's backbone.

It was early October, seventy-five days and 3,500-plus miles since I'd departed New Delhi, and part of me wished I were home. I missed talking with friends, sleeping in my own bed, cooking my own meals, sitting on my veranda, saying hello to my neighbors, and sipping tea with friends. The longing for that familiar world and the harshness of riding a motorcycle in India, of being alone, made me consider loading Kali on a train and heading home.

As appealing as the notion was, I didn't want to. I'd spent years embroidering my father's You-can-go-anywhere-do-anything-be-anyone message into my inner being, my identity, my *atman*, I needed to finish what I started. I needed another chapter in my can-do narrative, needed to finish rewriting the girl who clung to a wall and prove to her she was capable—capable of things beyond my wildest imaginings. There was only one way to go and that was forward on the path I'd set into motion.

काली

Just north of Rameswaram, Kali lurched and yipped as if something tugged her from behind. I pulled off the road and under the lacy shade of a eucalyptus tree. One of the saddlebag ties had come loose and gotten knotted in the chain. I freed it and set off again, but the jerking continued.

I hadn't been sleeping well and my mood teamed with frustration. Earlier that morning, I'd argued with a soldier at a border station assigned to prevent Sri Lanka's Tamil Tiger terrorists from slipping in. The guard had eased his rifle off his shoulder and gestured for me to remove my helmet and dupatta so he could see my face. The barrel wasn't aimed at me, but he held it in a manner that angered me, and I'd refused, removing only my sunglasses to show my cat-colored eyes—olive and gold like my father's. Unsatisfied, he motioned with the rifle for me to remove it all. The incident reminded me of a time in New Delhi when a police officer pulled me over for not wearing a helmet that I was clearly wearing. This soldier had no more reason to stop me than that officer, and we argued in our respective languages. The racket alerted a more senior guard who shambled out of a tent and waved me on.

Kali continued her primal screams and jerking, so I stopped again, near a walled village, to investigate the cause. Drumming and chanting drifted over the top of the smooth mud walls as I heaved Kali onto her center stand, thinking the tangled tie had loosened the chain and it needed tightening. Testing Nanna's philosophy—*India will provide*—I searched for brick or stone to prop under the stand so I could get the rear wheel in the air, but found nothing. The drumming stopped and I sensed I wasn't alone. Turning, I saw a couple of men from the village staring.

"Chain loose," I explained.

They nodded, as if I'd imparted some great insight, and repeated it to each other, "Chain loose. Chain loose." I unlocked the toolbox and retrieved my wrenches, then looked again for something to put under the stand to raise the rear wheel off the ground. One of the men understood what I was casting about for and said something to a woman who'd appeared, along with the rest of the villagers. She hustled off and I removed my jacket and helmet, causing a small stir among the growing crowd.

The woman returned with a large flat rock, and I awkwardly tried to wedge it under Kali's center stand without toppling her, as a couple of men rushed forward to help. With the stone in place, the men melted back into the crowd, and I picked up a wrench and squatted beside the wheel. From a distance, the men shouted instructions I couldn't understand, and probably wouldn't have listened to anyway, while shaking their heads and pointing their fingers in a flurry. I ignored them and continued to work the way Nanna had taught me.

When I finished, I looked at my greasy hands, and the woman who'd fetched the stone motioned for me to follow her into the village. She led me to an earthen bowl filled with clean water and another woman brought me a slither of blue soap. I hesitated to dirty the water. Water was a scarce resource and I didn't see a village well. Without one, the women and girls would have to fetch it from afar, carrying it back in buckets balanced on their heads. The women urged me on, smiling proudly as I washed up.

The villagers amassed behind us to witness my ablutions, then I turned and we all headed back to Kali. Donning my gear, I climbed on and kickstarted her to life, waving goodbye and thinking the problem solved. But as I gained speed, the shuttering and honking returned; when I slowed, it ceased.

I hadn't secured the toolbox and it fell open, scattering wrenches and screwdrivers onto the highway. Irritated and perplexed by the problem, I retrieved the tools and re-inspected Kali. I couldn't figure it out and decided to drive to the nearest town and find a mechanic. To prevent Kali from doing the Saint Vitus Dance, I kept her speed at an agonizingly slow twenty miles an hour.

An eternity later, I arrived in a hamlet and found a young mechanic slumped in a corner of a darkened shop. His flat, unfriendly expression dared me to bother him, but I needed a mechanic and explained the problem the best I could, figuring I hadn't done a decent job tightening the chain myself. After he worked on it, I test drove Kali and found the problem persisted. The mechanic pointed to the front shock and said, "Bad. Change it." But the problem wasn't in the front, it was in the rear. Before I could say this, he added, "Not me. Someone else."

A sign indicated the next town was fifteen miles north, a distance that would take more than an hour to cover at twenty miles per hour, but I had no choice. The bucking and screeching continued, each jolt pitching me forward. Several miles down the road, I spotted a truck parked on the side of the road. I hoped it wasn't broken down so I could hire the driver to take Kali and me to a mechanic. As I got closer, I saw the truck's hood was propped up and two men and a boy leering at the engine. I stopped anyway.

"How far to the next town?"

"Three kilometers, madam," said one of the men.

I lingered, hoping they'd miraculously fix their truck and I could get a lift, as a man puttered up on a small motorcycle. The men exchanged words, and the man waved at me and said, "Follow me. I take you to town."

As I trailed behind him, Kali bucked and honked like a goose. The noise caused him to crane his head around then drop behind me to assess the situation. I watched him in the rearview mirror, his face first quizzical then satisfied when he figured it out. Waving me to the side of the road, he pointed to the rear fender, lifted it from the tire and dropped it dramatically to illustrate the problem. The fender's screws had fallen out, causing it to create the stutter as it dragged across the rubber. He removed one of the saddlebag ties and threaded it through the fender's screw holes, knotting it to a strut as a temporary fix.

The man led me to a mechanic's shop at a dusty little crossing in the middle of nowhere. A kid-mechanic pulled a jar of screws and bolts down from a shelf and poured the contents onto the ground, picking through the assorted sizes until he found a suitable one. Despite his nimble fingers and slim hands, he struggled to reach and secure the bolts in the tight space between the wheel and the fender. When he finished, I asked how much I owed him, and he looked over at a band of whiskery old men hunched on a bench at the back of the shop who peered back wordlessly. They might have blinked Morse code, for he finally said, "Ten rupees."

I didn't have any small bills in my wallet and wasn't sure he could make change, so I looked around for a shop to break a hundred. The boy mistook my hesitation for a complaint and amended his fee, "Okay. Five rupees."

I shook my head and explained by holding up the hundred. He took it and trotted off for change. He returned and I handed him a twenty for his efforts, but he dug into his pocket and handed me ten rupees. I shook my head and he fretted, probably thinking I was paying him five rupees after all. A raspy voice said something from the shadows, one of the old men mumbling an explanation, and the boy grinned.

32

Planet Earth

The wheel debacle delayed me from reaching Punducherry as planned, so I spent the night in Thanjavur and arrived in Punducherry the next day, riding 123 miles of dusty road through villages bookended with obscure speed bumps and singing endless choruses of Jeremiah to combat the boredom. In Punducherry, I by-passed sherbet-colored hotels with scrolling wrought-iron balconies facing the ashen sea in favor of a place on the outskirts, a place my guidebook promised as "frequented by motorcyclists." I craved the company of riders to commiserate with on the hardships of the road, but there weren't any bikers when I arrived.

The motor lodge's courtyard appeared charming in the glow of lanterns laced through trees dripping with moss that shrouded a sprinkling of tables draped in checkered cloths. But the charm dissipated when the owner handed me a set of scratchy gray sheets and led me to a cinder block cell with a concrete slab for a bed, topped with a cheap foam pallet. Too tired to change hotels, I dumped my gear and gathered the few items I needed for a quick—cold—shower in the communal bathroom, then scampered back to my room wrapped in a thin lungi as a cloud of ravenous insects descended upon me. I dressed and returned to the cafe to join a couple of strung-out Westerners curled over cups of coffee and whispering among themselves. I ordered fish and chips since I was near the sea, and tried to work myself into a comfortable position, a futile attempt given the plastic furniture and my boney state.

There was something romantic and creepy about the courtyard, like a winsome secret garden containing a chalk outline of a murder victim. As my food arrived, I watched a corpulent white man stroll into the garden and sit at the next table. He ordered a King Fisher beer and looked over at me.

"Are you riding that Bullet? It's got Delhi plates," he said. "Did you ride it from Delhi by yourself?"

I nodded and he scooted over to join me without being invited.

"I'm Gene. My last name's 'Liberty,'" he said. "I changed it when I abandoned my separatist life in England for a spiritual one in Sri Aurobindo. Where are you from?"

I opened my mouth to speak, but he continued talking.

"I tell people I'm from Planet Earth," he said. "Planet Earth. Get it?"

I got it and wasn't sure I wanted anymore but quickly caught on that any hope of a tête-à-tête conversation was out of the question. I ate and nodded, drank coffee and nodded, as Gene monologued for an hour before he asked me another question.

"What do you do for a living?" he said.

It felt like a trick question. More about identity than income, so I simply said, "Journalist."

"I've always been tempted to tell people I'm an investigative journalist," he said, "because I like to ask so many questions."

My eyes widened, but he didn't notice. Instead, he expressed love for a woman named Linda he'd met on the plane to India and complained about life at an experimental lifestyle compound he was living at named Auroville. The commune, started in 1968 by a French woman known as The Mother, was an "experiment in international living where men and women could live in peace and progressive harmony."

"She's my soul mate," he said, referring to the woman from the plane, "and I've got to find her. I don't know her last name. All I know is she was on her way to Kolkata to work in Mother Teresa's orphanage."

Talking about her caused him to bounce excitedly in his chair as her image grew lovingly in his mind. I grew numb listening to him; my responses reduced to blinks. He was like some carnivorous creature that paralyzed its prey before devouring them.

"You must see Auroville," he said. "It's fantastic. I've got a great little hut in the middle of the forest, with a huge pink bathtub. It's nothing like this," he said, disdainfully waving a pudgy hand around. "I'll take you tomorrow."

I blinked like helpless prey, knowing there was no escape, and he took it as a yes.

काली

I was enjoying a cup of coffee the next morning when Gene sputtered up on a little motorcycle and plopped next to me. "I need coffee," he groaned, snapping his fingers for service.

I'd slept well, despite the primitive conditions of my room, but the calm evaporated when Gene appeared. He gulped his coffee and hopped up, insisting we go. Despite my dislike for Gene, he held some sort of Svengali powers I couldn't break free from. Besides, I was curious to see the compound and followed him back to Auroville on Kali.

On his 100cc, Gene—as-round-as-he-was-wide—reminded me of a circus bear on a bicycle as he expertly maneuvered the road's obstacles. When we arrived, Gene prattled on about the commune's design, culture, industriousness, internationality, and residents. He oozed on about how The Mother and her devotees transformed 2,500 acres of dying land into a lush green forest by planting more than two million fruit and fuel trees. At the center of the grounds was the Matri Mandir—a domed, dimpled meditation hall that resembled Disney World's Spaceship Earth.

"It's the ugliest thing I've ever seen," Gene said, leaping off his motorcycle.

I dismounted and headed for the door, but he stopped me. "It's not finished, so no one is allowed inside," he said. "The interior still needs to be filled with gold discs."

For the next half hour, he whirled me around the grounds, pointing out harvested rainwater, organic gardens, and research centers for alternative energy sources: wind, solar, biogas, and wastewater. While it interested me, his blather exhausted me. I wanted to return to my creepy little hotel and relax, but Gene had other plans.

"I need you to take me to town on your bike so I can pick up my Bullet," he said.

I hated the idea of this unctuous blowhard clinging to my back as we rode the few miles to Punducherry.

"Can't you ride the motorcycle you've been riding to get your Bullet?" I asked.

"That belongs to my neighbor."

"My passenger seat is really tiny," I countered, worried Kali would blow a tire with him on her too.

"I don't mind."

"You'd be more comfortable in a rickshaw."

"I'd rather ride with you."

I wanted to walk away, telling him "no," but my polite Midwestern upbringing wouldn't let me, so I grimaced and headed for Kali. Gene performed a little hop-and-hurdle act to get on, and I braced for his landing by squeezing the front brake and digging my heels into the ground. Kali bounced and I moaned, regretting not adjusting her suspension and tire pressure first.

"Let's go," he said, squirming to situate himself. "I need to get there before they close."

Concerned the extra weight would damage Kali's shocks if I drove fast, I kept the speed low.

"Do you always go this slow?" he asked, sounding disturbingly like Mukesh when we searched for my bag, and wiggling like him too, redirecting Kali with each shift. I upped the speed, eager to get him there and off Kali.

We arrived, and he slid gracefully off and scurried into the motorcycle shop, instructing me to wait while he checked on his Bullet. "After that, I want you to go with me to a carpet shop where I've got my eye on a Kashmiri carpet."

The carpet dealer greeted us—as he did thousands of Westerners who wandered into his shop—by voraciously pulling out carpets and instructing a boy to bring chai.

Gold and rose and cerulean carpets in traditional loopy patterns were plopped before us, much to Gene's dissatisfaction.

"No, no, no" he grumbled. "You know me. Show me the carpet *I* like."

The man nodded and continued slapping rugs on the heap. I wasn't sure if he recognized Gene and was searching for the one he wanted, or simply going through the same motions as he would with any other customer. The pile grew to knee level when Gene shouted, "That's it!"

I've looked at many carpets in Turkey and Kashmir, so I was familiar with the process of negotiations. But my experiences didn't match Gene's tactics as he shifted into a louder, monotone voice, reeling out each word solo.

"IF. I. BUY. I. ONLY. WANT. THIS. ONE. NO. OTHER. DO. YOU. UNDERSTAND?"

Gene turned to me, "He told me it's all hand-knotted, and it took five months to make. It's real raw silk."

The shopkeeper started a new pile, flopping one carpet after another onto the floor. "You like this one? Which size you want? I have many. All sizes. Tell me. What size you want?"

"NO. NO. I. ONLY. WANT.... " Gene started again.

My head throbbed, and I said I was going outside. On the shop's steps, I watched the traffic whiz past. People shopping and heading home from work wove between traffic with bags on their heads or in their hands. Cars, buses, and rickshaws stirred up dust and blasting horns urged pedestrians to hurry. Among the swirling chaos, I saw a man in a polyester suit stoop in the middle of the road to scoop up sugar that had spilled from his broken bag. He swiftly gathered the crystals, oblivious to the trucks and scooters zipping precariously close to his head. As he did, an old woman in a limp white sari watched him from the edge of the road, her hollow eyes tracking his frantic hands. When he finished and retreated from the road, she eased out into the traffic to collect the remaining bits of the sweetness, gathering the fine grains and dribbling her reward into a pouch she'd fashioned in her sari's pallu.

The next morning, I spread my maps on a table and ordered a pot of tea. As I planned my route to Mamallapuram, a seventh-century port city, Gene strolled in and plunked down beside me.

"Where are you going?" he asked.

If I told him, he'd insist on coming with me, and this was a solo trip. Instead of lying as I wanted, I heard myself say, "Mamallapuram."

"I'll come with you. I need to break-in my Bullet's engine."

A little voice inside insisted I speak up and say I didn't want him with me, but the look on his face, of a kid who knew he wasn't wanted, kept the words from coming out. I didn't want to be unkind and he seemed so pathetic. If the road taught me anything, it was what it was like to long for human companionship. I said I was leaving at six, secretly hoping he'd find it too early and I'd be justified in leaving without him.

33

Eaten Alive

Gene tooted his horn at 5:45 a.m., as I finished my coffee. This was my trip, and I'd be damned if I'd allow him to dictate it, so I ordered another coffee, hoping he'd grow impatient and leave without me. But he only honked his horn several more times before bounding into the courtyard.

"Thought you wanted to go at six?" he asked, spilling into the chair next to me.

I closed my eyes and wished him away as he launched into a description of all he'd packed for the trip. Ridiculous, I thought, at least on the road I wouldn't have to listen to him.

Gene raced his Bullet ahead while I dallied behind, riding as slow as I could to keep as much distance as possible between us. The morning light filtered over the fields, massaging the land awake and refracting through dew drops dangling from blades of sweet grass and prickly bushes. Women and girls walked along the edge of the road carrying empty pails and jugs for water, as I stewed about Gene. Forgetting that speed bumps bookended southern villages, I hit one, startling me. Gene watched from the side of the road, where he waited for me to catch up, snickering at my misfortune. I slowed, knowing he wouldn't be able to stand the wait and would ride on.

The turn for Mamallapuram came without warning, and I saw Gene fly past it. My good-self considered trying to catch him, but my not-so-good self stopped me. He'd figure it out, and I wasn't obligated to him, I thought, hearing my mother's voice say, "That isn't nice." I pulled to the side of the road and waited for him to return. He flew past me and into town. I found him in the parking lot of the blue hotel.

"I'm staying here," he said, leaning Easy Rider-like against his motorcycle.

This was my opportunity to ditch him without seeming mean, having already planned to stay at another hotel.

"You took so long getting here that I've already checked in," he said, "I'm in room nine."

"I'm staying at the Rama Krishna down the street," I said, confident it was safe to say now that he'd booked a room. "It has a covered parking area." A vexed little voice in me yelped, *What's wrong with you? Shut up. Don't sell him on the place.* But it was too late.

"Where is it? What does it look like?" he prodded, climbing back on his motorcycle. "I think I'll come check it out too."

You are a fool, I berated myself.

I arrived at the hotel to glimpse Gene dashing up the stairs with a hotel worker in tow. U-shaped, the hotel hugged an inviting courtyard that all the rooms faced, and possessed a clean, welcoming fresh feel. Gene darted along the balcony from room to room, the employee barely keeping up, while a second clerk showed me a commodious corner room with a double bed and two windows offering cross ventilation. I opened my mouth to say, "I'll take it," when Gene thundered in.

"This is perfect," he said, pirouetting to survey the room. "I'll take it."

"No, you won't," I hissed, relieved to hear I'd found my voice. "You said you were staying at the Tina Blue."

I expected him to fuss and bully, but he simply shrugged. "Okay, okay. Fair enough. I'll take that one," he said, pointing to a room across the courtyard. "It only cost seventy-five rupees, so I can save money."

I wouldn't be able to stand being in the same hotel and thought I'd have to look elsewhere when he flip-flopped again, saying he'd stay at Tina Blue after all.

"I'll be back in half an hour. We'll go to breakfast," he shouted over his shoulder as he danced down the stairs.

We sat in an endearing little cafe at a table next to an arched window cascading in ivy bursting from terra cotta pots. As my omelet, toast, and coffee arrived, Gene leaned across the table.

"Did you notice how unhappy those guys at your hotel were when I left?" he said. "It's because they figured out we weren't a couple, and I was going to take a room on my own. They thought, 'Here's our chance.' But then I left."

"Chance for what?" I asked, forking golden, cheesy egg into my mouth.

"It's obvious. They fancied me."

I'd stopped paying attention to what Gene said because most of it was nonsense, but I nearly choked on this revelation. "Fancied you?" I said.

"Sure. I've been propositioned enough in this country to know when someone fancies me. It happens all the time."

I stared at him unsure if he was kidding or being serious, as he continued making wild proclamations about men wanting him, including the 'eye' the waiters were giving him at that moment. I escaped his drivel by tuning him out and gazing at the street scene below. Mamallapuram looked lovely. The sun slanted just so, kissing the wind chimes hanging in the shops below as a breeze stirred them and ruffled ladies' saris. Gene poked the last bit of his omelet into his mouth. "I could eat all day," he said, leaning back in his chair and slapping his belly

I nodded and pushed back my chair, "Catch you later."

"Where are you going?"

"The post office." Damn, there I went again.

"I'll go with you."

After handing my letters to a dour postal clerk who canceled the stamps and tossed them into a bin behind him, I headed toward the beach—Gene at my side. The beach was empty except for a few fishing nets, encrusted with dead crabs. I didn't want to be alone with Gene listening to his crazy talk, so I steered him to the souvenir shops and struck up a conversation with a shopkeeper. Gene didn't care for conversations that weren't about him and lurked sullenly up and down the aisles before announcing he needed some rest and strode off down the street. I continued to wander in and out of the shops for a bit longer but being with Gene had drained me and I returned to my hotel for a midday nap. An hour later, as I dozed on my soft bed, the door open for more air, Gene showed up bemoaning how he'd been "woken up by some loud Brit complaining."

"Imagine that," I murmured.

"Sorry. Sorry. SORRY," he said, bowing and backing out of the room, coming to a rest against the balcony.

There were sites I wanted to see in Mamallapuram, so I got up. The day had cooled as I headed to the 1,400-year-old stone carvings of Arjuna's Penance. It's an epic scene from the

Mahabharata depicting India's dualistic culture—male/female, birth/death, good/bad—seeing things as both/and, rather than either/or. The carvings told a flood story showing pairs of animals—elephants, deer, tigers, man, and more—chiseled into prehistoric rock.

We followed the narrow dirt road winding through Mamallapuram toward the temples. The hawkers and vendors shouted, "Hello, madam" and "Hello, sir," hoping to lure us in. Gene barreled down the middle of the road, ignoring traffic and shouting, "Fuck you, you bastards," at autorickshaw drivers who blasted their horns at him. I cringed each time and mourned the loss of what should have been a pleasant experience at one of the world's most impressive man-made monuments. By the time I sloughed myself free of Gene an hour later, I'd lost my appetite for experiences and developed a headache.

काली

Gene pounded on my door the next morning at dawn. I could not take another day of him but didn't want to say it to his face either, so I ignored him, hoping he'd go away. Gene was a pest, but I was more frustrated and angrier with myself for not taking charge of the situation from the start. It was a weakness, but also a kindness. I didn't want to hurt his feelings. I felt sorry for him. I'd gotten to know Gene a little bit and sympathized with his loneliness. Even in his bravado, he was vulnerable, and I related to that. I kept hearing my mother's voice in my head telling me how she was treated by others as a kid because she was poor and didn't fit in; how she hoped her children never shunned anyone. But Gene was suffocating.

I sensed Gene's face pressed against the screen window, and pretended to be asleep. The windows were open, but I'd drawn the gauzy curtains before going to bed. I heard him shuffling about, searching for a gap to peek through. Sure he could sense I was faking it, I held my breath as he forced his face into the mesh.

After a while, he turned and retreated. I didn't dare move, making sure he was good and gone before I stirred. When I sat up, I saw he'd pushed an envelope under the door. Inside was a note and the thirty rupees he'd borrowed the day before. The note said he was going to find Linda, the soul mate he'd met on the plane. I smiled wickedly. No more Gene meant things were looking up.

34

Cults and Curses

I had twenty-five days and 2,400 miles to reach Kolkata by October 30, Kali Puja. A little tighter timeframe than the last time I'd calculated but still doable, so I decided to stay an extra day for the festivities now that Gene is gone.

Mamallapuram crackled with people preparing for the holy day to honor Sarasvati, the goddess of learning and music. The guys operating the hotel told me everything had to be scrubbed clean—houses, hotels, vehicles—and decorated, instructing me to do the same for Kali. Aside from being caught in the occasional rainstorm, I'd not washed her since leaving New Delhi and she looked as rough as I did. I thought the cleansing could purify my spirits too, rinsing all the residual bad juju lingering in me from recent events: Gene, hijras, old man on the street, Kiara. But especially Samar, and the way that ended.

The hotel guys gave me a bucket of water and soap to wash Kali before they whizzed through the rooms with brooms, dabbing the door frames with saffron and vermillion to invite wealth, longevity, and wellness. When I finished my work, I set out in search of a marigold garland to drape over Kali's headlamp, a "must" if I was to ingratiate myself with the goddess Sarasvati.

The morning felt fresh with the perpetual dust tamped down by taxis and autorickshaws being doused with water. The streets were brisk with people popping in and out of shops. As I passed one shop, a wasp-thin guy with a shaved head wearing an oversized T-shirt invited me to join him for a cup of coffee. His English was impeccable with an accent that sounded West Indian, but he said he was from Punducherry as he introduced himself as Gangol. His sparse shop had one display case that filled the front of the tiny store and housed a collection of a dozen or so items. At first, he said he owned the shop, then he said he worked for the owner and was the artisan of the stonework, mostly chillums for smoking dope, but also carved paperweights and crudely-painted illustrations of Indian moguls. I doubted he was the owner or the artisan but I wasn't going to argue. The day was too lovely to be spoiled.

"Things just come to me," he said, rocking on folded legs as we settled onto the floor. "If I think I want a watch, that afternoon I will be walking on the beach and I will find a beautiful watch lying in the sand."

I groaned inwardly, wondering what was it about me that attracted loonies. *Get up and go now*, I told myself, wondering how best to do that.

"I don't know why," Gangol continued, his eyes bouncing about the room as if seeking the answer in a secret message. "Once I was thinking, 'It is my birthday and I would like a new pair of jeans.' Later, I was sitting in a restaurant having chai with my friend when an English couple walked in. They always visit me when they are in India. They say, 'Gangol, it is your birthday and we have a gift for you.' I opened the bag and inside I find a new pair of jeans."

I nodded.

"I did not ask. I was just thinking," he said, tittering to himself and twirling a stick across the floor. "It comes to my mind, and then it comes to me. Whatever I am thinking comes true."

He droned on and I faded until he mentioned Kali. "I worship Kali. She is very powerful. Maybe that is where my power comes. Maybe Kali gives me the gift. Sometimes I have dreams...." He broke off, rocking sinisterly with a numinous expression. "Sometimes I think I'm mad. Why am I singled out for special powers? Do you know? Do you know why I am special?"

I shook my head and sneaked a look at my watch.

"Are you going to Kolkata?" he asked.

"I'm headed that way," I said cautiously.

"Will you take a letter to the Kali temple for me?"

The guy was unhinged but maybe he was put in my path for a reason, a means of redeeming some good karma for my own transgressions.

"Sure," I said, seizing the moment to leave. "I'll come back later and pick it up."

"Wait. I want to give you something. Something I made myself," he rocked and snickered for a few moments, as if in some ethereal consultation, before crawling over to the display case to rummage in a drawer and pulling out a simple, smooth chillum. I thanked him, took it (even though I didn't smoke dope), and left him giggling and swaying on the floor.

I planned to leave early the next day and returned to the hotel to pack, burying the chillum deep among my socks in the saddlebags. When I was finished, one of the hotel clerks helped me decorate Kali by appropriately dotting her with sindoor and saffron to her auspicious parts: headlight, front fender, gas tank, toolboxes, rear fender, and gearbox. As I laced two strands of amber and crimson marigolds around the handlebars, the clerk asked where my banana leaves were.

"I couldn't find any," I said.

"Everyone will have them on their autos," he said, looking stricken. Unsure why this faux pas rated such concern, I waited for him to explain. Finally, he said, "It is okay. You will be safe."

काली

There is no accounting for crazy because I returned to Gangol's shop that evening to pick up the letter as promised. Inside a shuddering candle illuminated a small iron statue of the goddess Sarasvati with offerings of apples and oranges and spikes of patchouli sticks, their smoke curling musically in the air around it. Bollywood tunes reverberated from neighboring shops. People passed by Gangol's but none stopped. I stood at the doorframe hoping he'd simply hand me the letter, but my luck was of a different sort.

"Come. Come," he said, waving me inside.

"Just for a moment. I can't stay," I said, wary of his mercurial moods. "Do you have the letter ready?"

"I thought we could eat dinner together."

"I can't." I lied. "I have work to do."

"You promised."

"I promised to pick up your letter," I said tersely, determined not to get sucked into another cannibalizing Gene-like situation.

"It will only take a minute to write. Sit down. Have some fruit," he said, plucking an apple from Sarasvati's bounty. "I have another gift for you," he said, pulling down one of the scroll paintings. I wanted nothing to do with him or from him but took it to keep the peace, hoping it would speed things along.

The candles flickered in the warm breeze as Gangol fussed over the fruit display and made no attempt to produce a letter for Kali Mata.

"What is your hurry?" he said. "I thought you were having dinner with me. That is why I did not eat all day."

I repeated my need to leave, but it made no difference.

"I am lucky to be so special," he said, squatting on his heels and pitching back and forth in the guttering candlelight. "You know, I have a gift. Whatever I think comes to me."

"If you write the letter, I'll be glad to take it with me," I said, that little voice in me protesting, *Why aren't you walking away?*

"I feel sorry for others who do not have my gift. Why am I like this? Why am I special?" He paused and chortled, then added, "I think I am mad."

"The letter?"

He shot me a sharp look. "It will only take a minute," he said, drifting into another world in his mind. "I saw an angel. I want to have a daughter. I will call her Angel."

"I need to go," I said, inching back to the door.

"If you do not want to have a meal with me, at least have a juice," he snapped, then, in a softer, sadder tone added, "It is on the way back to where you are staying. I will write the letter at the restaurant. I really want you to take it, if you still will."

I didn't remember telling him where I was staying, and the thought of him knowing felt threatening. But I reminded myself that locals always seemed to know this stuff. Once, my former landlords in New Delhi came to visit me at my new apartment in another colony across town. When they couldn't find my home, they asked a vendor pushing a cart if he knew and he'd directed them where the "woman with long blond hair" lived.

Gangol was insane. If he knew where I was staying, I didn't know what he might do if he didn't get his way. I kept repeating, *Whatever's wrong with him you can handle. It will be over soon.*

On the way to get juice, Gangol continued his gibberish, telling me he hadn't seen himself in a mirror in years. "Some people have to look at themselves in mirrors all the time. But I do not know what my face looks like," he said.

A large mirror hung in the restaurant's entryway and Gangol stopped, stepped back, and leaned over to examine himself, preening and smiling at his image. I choked back the urge to point out the lie. He looked truly disturbed.

At the table, he complained again that I promised to eat with him and how he didn't want to eat alone. I refused to be guilted into eating, recalling Mark Twain's advice, "Never argue with a fool, onlookers may not be able to tell the difference."

"Go, if you are in such a hurry. Leave. I don't need you to take my letter."

That's all I needed, I realized. I'd been waiting for permission to abandon him, waiting to be relieved of my Midwestern obligations. I stood and dropped some rupees on the table for the juice a waiter had just delivered.

"I do not need your money," Gangol shouted.

"It's for the waiter," I called over my shoulder.

"Hey you," he hissed. "You are nothing to ME."

His malicious tone drove through me, and I quickened my pace. *Get away. Get away. Get away*, I chanted as I hurried toward the darkness. I slipped outside and into the street, my heart thudding as he called, "Hey, you forgot the letter," he said pleasantly. "It was nice to meet you."

In the street, I realized I still clutched the ridiculous painting he gave me. It burned my hand and I searched for someone to foist it on. Two lone figures floated toward me. As we passed, I thrust the scroll at the little girl walking with an old woman, relieved to be rid of my connection to Gangol.

35

Naked on the Edge

I leaned Kali hard into the curve, her pegs scraped the asphalt in the apex as the wind whipped the ends of my dupatta into a frantic flutter of red and green, tugging at my concentration like a warning. The highway was eerily empty. No cars. No buses. No trucks. No pedestrians ambled along the edge of the road. Only a barren landscape surrounded me as Kali's ccs shimmied up my spine. Beneath me, the highway blurred like a ghost and behind me, Mamallapuram thinned away as bits of gravel and seeds pinged my wrists. I shrugged off the niggling doomsday feeling that chased me like the wind and rolled on the throttle. Gaining speed, I wished for another curve to cure the monotony of the road spooling endlessly ahead. Dust swirled under Kali's wheels and mingled with the smell of sweet grass. The collar of my jacket tapped my helmet like an insistent finger. Any omen the gods conveyed came too late. In the middle of the road stood a boy straddling a bike with one leg hooked under the bar of a too-big bicycle.

Our eyes locked as the distance between us shrank and time suspended. His face lifted in surprise and eyes widened in excitement. My motorcycle instructors taught me to look in the direction I wanted to go. I knew I'd hit him if I didn't look away. But I couldn't tear my eyes from his bandy legs or birdlike ribcage. His impossibly frail cotton singlet was his sole defense to my steel.

I didn't hear the squall of rubber, didn't hear the screams, didn't feel the impact. Caught up in the crooning voice of Lyle Lovett singing in my ears through earphones from a cassette in my pocket, I didn't see the boy until it was too late to stop, I had to swerve.

But I didn't. Instead, I panicked, stomped the brakes and hit the boy's bike, flipping Kali and sending her skittering down the road.

I must have shut my eyes because I don't remember hitting the boy. I only remember coming to, flat on my back, unable to breathe as someone tugged at my helmet. I wasn't alone.

Whoever had tugged at my helmet returned a second time and I swiped at them to go away as I struggled to breathe. I could have a broken neck or cracked vertebra, tugging my helmet could sever and snap my spine. Paralyze me.

I cautiously moved my head and opened my eyes, glimpsing blurry figures moving about me. I strained to hear the boy, praying I hadn't killed him. Screwed into an unnatural pose on the pavement, I was afraid to move. Each breath I inhaled seared my lungs, and I feared they might be punctured.

Checking for broken bones, I carefully moved my arms, waving each independently. Then, with the help of someone I couldn't see, I pushed myself into an upright position. My legs stretched before me akimbo, giving me the comical notion of a cartoon character flattened by a steamroller. The thought of a truck hurtling along and making it a reality motivated me to try and move. "Please don't let me die on the side of this road," I begged.

Panting, I managed to oxygenate my brain enough to keep it from panicking as I listened again for the boy. A soft moan drifted to me. I tried to turn my head in the direction of the sound but couldn't. Needing to get up, I leaned back on my hands to assess my body's damage. My right leg was bent away from me and my left twisted in the opposite direction. There was a hole in my jean's right knee. Something had punctured the cloth —a rock perhaps—and blood seeped from the opening while my knee swiftly ballooned.

I rolled my legs carefully back to normal positions and ran my hands down them, sickened by the possibility of broken bones. I wiggled my ankles and gingerly raised each leg a bit. Both moved enough to assure me nothing was broken.

Nausea rose in me, and I feared I'd throw up inside my helmet so I pulled it off. Once free of my lifesaver, my vision steadied enough to see Kali lying on her side some twenty yards in front of me, the result of a low-side. Luckily, she'd skidded in front of me, as opposed to a highside, where I'd have been pitched over the handlebars and had 500 pounds of hot metal chasing me.

The previously desolate highway now overflowed with people, and I wondered where they'd come from. I hadn't noticed a village before the crash, but dozens of people crept out of the parched land to help. Two women bent and picked up my things —camera bag, books, pens, maps, water bottle, and more— littering the highway. A couple of men lifted Kali from a pool of gasoline trickling from her tank. She seemed to roll okay.

I eased myself around and saw the boy stretched out near me and watched the steady rise and fall of his fragile ribcage. I didn't see any blood, but that didn't mean his injuries weren't bad. I needed to clear my head enough think of what to do next. My befuddled mind conjured up a story a woman told me about an accident she and her boyfriend had on their motorcycle in northern India. They'd crashed into the back of a bull-ox cart and rammed the pole on the cart into the back of the old man driving it. Villagers witnessing the incident pulled the couple from their bike and beat them. I worried the same could happen to me. My crime was worse than hitting an old man. I hit a boy. Boys were India's future.

"Come, madam," said a man, holding out a hand to help me up. Another joined him and together they lifted and lead me off the highway. My right leg wouldn't bend, so the men helped me hobble to a tea stall at the road's edge. The sight of the chai wallah's stall and village huts fanning behind it rattled me. How could I have been so oblivious to miss seeing an entire village? A dozen people gathered in knots to watch me as the men guided me to a charpoy. The boy now rested on a straw mat nearby, his eyes closed and his mouth slack. I wanted to ask about his condition but breathing shredded my lungs.

Two old women in threadbare saris shooed the men aside and eased me down onto the charpoy. One of them held up my purple daypack, shaking it to show me my stuff was safe. The zipper busted in the impact and the flap hung uselessly open, but they'd carefully collected and returned its contents.

"*Thik hai. Thik hai,*" said one of them, smiling and bobbling her head as she patted the pack as if it were a child. Theft was the last thing on my mind but the first on hers and the others. As a Western woman alone on the road I must have struck them as imposing. They might have feared the repercussions a foreigner could bring to them, much like I'd feared from them.

The chai wallah's kettle bubbled next to him as smoke from the wood fire filled the stall and stung my eyes. The woman with my pack moved to the end of the charpoy and unlaced my boots while the other one sat next to me soothing my face with the end of her pallu that she dipped into a tin vessel of cool water. Their kind faces were deeply creased from years in the sun. The woman washing my face smiled down, showing a toothless maw. Their mothering of the boy and me made me long for my mom's touch, driving home how alone I really was.

A commotion kicked up outside the hut as people passing in cars, motorcycles, and scooters stopped to inquire about the crash. A few curious souls shuffled in to stare at me. The dark faces of men scrutinized my prone body, like medical students in Thomas Eakin's *The Gross Clinic*.

I refused to look at my injuries, but the women tending me relished showing me off and enthusiastically beaconed shadowy figures hovering in the door to come closer. Working in tandem, one of the old women hooked her bony finger into the tear in my jeans and pulled the fabric aside while the other directed onlookers to appraise the gnawed flesh inside, while I laid as helpless as a fish yanked from a lake.

Periodically, someone loomed over me and said, "Police coming." I wondered if I was going to be arrested. I hoped they'd take charge and help the boy and me get medical attention. A young man dressed in a black and white Polo shirt popped in. I thought he might speak English and asked about the boy's condition. From time to time, the boy and I had turned our heads toward each other, and our eyes met. His eyes held nothing I could read or expected to see—accusation, apprehension, reproach—just benign acceptance.

189

"Boy is *thik hai*. Only a small injury on his arm. That is all," said the guy, peering strangely at me, my freak status returning, before disappearing into the swell of people outside the hut.

I was concerned about the boy's injuries, but more worried about my own. Both knees throbbed, but my right was puffed up and strained my pant leg. Each breath scorched my lungs, worrying me that ribs could be broken. And, despite the helmet, I knew I'd sustained a concussion of some degree. The boy had a family to care for him. I was alone. No one knew where I was nor could they help if they did. I needed to stay strong and care for myself.

36

Ruined Program

I had no idea how much time passed before the man on the Kawasaki arrived. Half an hour? Forty-five minutes? Two hours? I drifted woozily in and out of awareness. When he pushed into the center of observers, the ladies attending me shrank away. He was in his forties with coal-black hair salted at the temples and a rash of stubble on his harsh face.

"My name is Chetan," he said, with such authority I thought he was the police. "You must go to Madras hospital."

Time may have escaped me but the memory of Madras' chaotic traffic hadn't. I could not manage Kali in its crushing environment in my condition. "It's too far. Isn't there a doctor closer?"

"My program is to go to Madras," he replied, referring to his day's agenda in the Indian vernacular as his *program*. "Not going to Madras ruins my program."

I'd made a promise to myself at the start of the journey to always go forward; returning to Madras was backtracking. Besides, it had been more than an hour since the wreck, and I was beginning to think my injuries were not as bad as I first feared.

"I'm not going to Madras," I said, fueled by the sugary chai the women had funneled into me.

Chetan stared scowling at me, shook his head, turned, and walked away grumbling, "My whole program is ruined."

I looked at the boy on the mat, then down at my ravaged right leg. *His* program was ruined?

The teen in the Polo returned and tugged at my arm, saying I was being taken to a nearby doctor. The ladies rushed to my side and nudged his hands away, saying something to me I couldn't understand but imagined was, "Come dear. We will help you."

My body had stiffened significantly since the accident and my engorged knee strained the jean seams so much it was impossible to bend. Chetan wheeled his Kawasaki near the tea stall, its little engine buzzing like an angry wasp. He looked put upon and impatient. "Town is just there," he said, pointing to a distant brown lump. "There will be a doctor."

I hesitated, pinned upright between the ladies and woozy as blood zig-zagged through my body, not because I didn't know him or where I'd be taken—I had little choice—but because I wondered how the boy would get to the doctor.

"Is there room for both the boy and me?" I asked, knowing whole families rode on motorcycles in India.

"Boy is not coming. His people will care for him," Chetan said. "You must come with me."

When I didn't immediately move, he groused, "My whole program is ruined."

"The boy needs medical attention too," I insisted.

"His people know what to do for him. You are a foreigner. The doctor is for you."

A doctor in the middle of nowhere was there for me? That didn't make sense.

"I'll pay for the boy to see the doctor. I want him to see a doctor."

"Boy's problem is bicycle. Destroyed," he said. "Who will pay for bike?"

"I'll pay for the bike and the doctor."

"Okay. Okay. Boy will come later. Chalo."

Sure he was lying but powerless to do anything about it, I wobbled over to his motorcycle—apprehensive about leaving Kali and all my stuff. As if clairvoyant, Chetan said, "Take care of your things. There are thieves."

How could I? I was leaving them behind.

The two women intuitively understood my distress and assured me with "*thik hai?*" and rocking heads that my belongings were secure. I trusted them but not the boy in the Polo shirt skulking about.

The women held my waist as Mr. Polo-Shirt commanded, and I steady myself by holding his shoulder with one hand as I lifted my damaged knee and leg up and over the saddle with my other hand. Swooning as I did, I managed to ease myself down and hook my heel on the bike's foot peg seconds before Chetan abruptly motored us away.

He stopped at the police station where two officers sat on chairs at the compound's shady entrance. The three exchanged words and a round-faced officer smiled and nodded at me while the thin one walked around the bike to investigate my throbbing knee. Waves of nausea rolled through me as the pain in my knee pulsed. I waited for someone to hustle me inside the station, but the conversation seemed too jovial. The police didn't care about the crash, and the boy was of no concern to them either. Chetan was simply showing me off, like some prize.

I tapped his shoulder, angry he'd made me a spectacle, and said, "I'm going to throw up if you don't get moving."

"Yes, yes. Of course," he said, sounding as if it was his idea, shifting the motorbike abruptly into gear and causing the officer to stumble back.

Chetan wasn't from the area, so he didn't know the location of the doctor's office. He trolled down one barren street after another, attempting to ask the few souls out for directions. It was easily 110 Fahrenheit, and the village didn't have a single shade tree. Most of the people ignored him, but one man proffered some directions that Chetan rejected, shaking his head and shouting "American doctor" as we buzzed away. Woozy from the heat and trauma, I couldn't imagine more than one doctor in the area let alone one for foreigners only.

We finally found the doctor's office—two small rooms at the back of a nondescript building. Every joint, muscle, tendon, nerve, vein, bone crackled in protest as I slid off the motorbike and tottered toward the door. A plump nurse bound in a blue sari steered me past a clutch of poor villagers crowded in the reception. They stared miserably at me as I clumped by in the wake of the nurse's swishing sari. She led me to a room and instructed me onto an exam table draped with a sheet splattered in bodily fluids. Another nurse joined us and they whispered with Chetan in the corner. I knew what they were talking about even without the smattering of English words like motorcycle and bicycle. As he dispensed the last detail of the crash, Chetan added his now familiar refrain, "My whole program is ruined," and the nurses commiserated with his woes.

37

Doctor, Doctor

The doctor didn't come to me in the examination room, rather I was shuffled into his office. Chetan helped me dodder over and eased me onto a chair while the doctor, a soft, fleshy looking middle-aged man, perched on his desk, waiting for me to be settled. The only indication of his professional status was his white lab coat, but I knew from experience that didn't guarantee he was the physician. A couple of years earlier, I broke a tooth eating fried chicken in Jaisalmer. The restaurant manager wrote down the name of a dentist and directions to her office, but when I arrived, a man entered the room, selected a shiny sharp instrument, and without introduction said, "Open wide." I knew the dentist was a woman and refused to open my mouth.

Without eye contact, greeting, or an assuring smile, the doctor brutishly pressed and wiggled my right kneecap. The probing didn't hurt much, which was a good sign, but I watched his expression closely for concern. I saw nothing. His face remained disturbingly emotionless throughout his thirty-second exam. Satisfied with his findings, he opened a drawer and retrieved a pair of shears more suitable for trimming hedges. Meeting my eyes for the first time, he wordlessly slipped the tip of the scissors into the hole and split the pant leg seam to seam. Inserting hard fingertips into the gap, he cruelly explored my flesh. I didn't know if he knew I'd hit a boy or if he was simply a hateful person. His prodding and poking made me feel more like an animal than a human.

From the opening in my jeans, I saw the gouge—a blackened crater pitted with gravel covered with scrim of congealed blood. The doctor jiggled my kneecap without pain rocketing through my body, so I didn't think it was fractured. He turned to his nurse and murmured something, prompting her to about-face out of the room and return with a stainless steel tray bearing a huge hypodermic needle. I knew about dirty needles in developing countries and carried disposable syringes from the United States for this kind of occasion. But my needles did me no good since they were in Kali's saddlebag at the crash site.

"No," I said, shaking my head.

The doctor surveyed me, surmising my level of insufferable stupidity, then waved the nurse away and took a bottle of antiseptic from a shelf. He splashed the stingy liquid onto a gauze square and taped it to my knee, not bothering to clean the debris imbedded in my ragged flesh. Finishing the task, he spoke his first and only words to me.

"Twenty rupees."

I stared back. My ribs hurt and I surely had a concussion—since I'd been knocked out—but he didn't bother examining me for other injuries, ignoring the abrasions on my elbow and left knee.

I didn't quibble with the fee, even though his doctoring didn't deserve the few rupees he charged. I fished the money from my wallet, as the doctor pulled out a prescription pad and wrote a script for pain pills. I handed him the money, but he pointed at his nurse with his pen, haughtily indicating I give it to her.

I'd lost track of Chetan, who'd disappeared during the examination, so the nurse in the swishing sari escorted me back to the original exam room, where Chetan sat in a chair cradling an orange soda. "Drink this," he said, thrusting the cold bottle at me.

My stomach churned and legs screeched as I scooted myself up onto the soiled sheets. I needed the energy the sugary soda provided for the ride back to the village. As I sipped, Chetan sat in the corner looking small and uncomfortable, his need to leave apparent, his "program" drifting further from reality as the day ticked by. His repeated mention of his "program being ruined" started sounding like a request for money, and I felt my self hardening to the thought.

After fifteen minutes, I felt strong enough to struggle onto his motorbike. I thought of the boy who hadn't come to this doctor and knew he was better off not coming here.

Back at the village, I got a good look at Kali's damage: scrapes and scratches on her tank, and the front fender slightly crumpled. Besides the spilled gas and the bent fender, she appeared undamaged.

Chetan commanded my keys and started Kali, who roared immediately. He ordered a village boy to fetch a mechanic to inspect and ensure Kali was ridable and fix her fender.

"Check your items," Chetan ordered. "Things may be missing."

Panic seized me as I remembered my camera and lenses. I poked around and discovered them still there and intact, but small things were missing: my alarm clock, the bundle of incense I carried to clear the stink from hotel rooms, my sunglasses, and my Walkman with my favorite Lyle Lovett cassette. I knew the women who'd cared for me hadn't taken the things but had an idea who had: Mr. Polo-Shirt. He'd held my jacket with the cassette player in the pocket when he'd lent me his shoulder so I could climb on Chetan's bike. He'd looked and acted shiftlessly, and now he and my music were gone.

38

Highway Robbery

The mechanic worked on Kali while people continued to insist the police were coming. I knew I couldn't stay there in the middle of nowhere much longer. I needed a hotel room to rest and to recover from the trauma. Since leaving the doctor's office, Chetan had turned attentive, dropping his mantra of "ruined program" and insisting I come to his house to heal.

"You will have a private room," he said, "and my wife will care for you."

I longed to leave, but nothing had been done for the boy yet. Aside from the scrape on his elbow, he appeared okay. His bike, however, was a mess, the front tire nearly folded in half.

The villagers clustered about Chetan and me insisting something be done for the boy, leading him out of the tea hut and into the circle. Standing him in front of me, they knitted closer and waited for a tall white woman to bestow justice to a small brown boy. His eyes were glassy and wary as if I might strike him. As if the crash were his fault.

"Give him 100 rupees," Chetan said.

I looked at Chetan; it was implausible to think two dollars would fix things. The villagers pushed closer, choking off the air.

Their expressions didn't convey hate but instead a weariness of beaten-down souls.

"No. No money. Police coming," said one man, still believing that doing the right thing meant the authorities should handle it. I'd met those authorities. They were not coming.

I wondered if the boy's parents were in the crowd. He stood as if he belonged to them all. I stood next to Chetan, knowing I was utterly alone, and not knowing what to do.

"One hundred rupees will fix the bike," Chetan said, his harsh tone striking the word "fix" like a hammer.

Twenty rupees would fix the bike, but that wasn't the point. Fixing the bike wasn't the issue. The men in the group grumbled, speaking all at once, including Chetan, raising their voices over each other until they reached a consensus.

"Okay, give him 150 rupees," Chetan said, but I suspected that wasn't what the villagers wanted. They wanted something money couldn't buy. They wanted justice. Justice not only for the incident but for something none of us could name.

In a way, I felt history heaped her ghostly self on me and I strained under her heartlessness. The boy and I knew we didn't have a say in the matter. His home, I imagined, slept half a dozen or more people on a dirt floor, and had no electricity or running water. He and his family likely managed to survive on a dollar a day. The world wasn't fair. I reached for my wallet.

"Do NOT show the money in wallet," Chetan hissed. "They will demand more."

"I can give more," I protested. "I want to give more."

"No. No money," said a man. "Police coming."

The boy's questioning eyes scanned the crowd, while those around him nodded assuringly. They seemed to be encouraging him to take whatever money was offered. But how could I justify paying him a few dollars? I was a foreigner. I had money and could afford to pay, but what was the right price for hitting the boy? Would a dollar amount fix the problem? What exactly was broken? The boy in some way I couldn't comprehend? The bike? Or was it something else—not what had been broken by the crash, but what was about to be broken? Was some bond or trust, an obligation between rich and poor, brown and white on the verge of shattering?

One-hundred and fifty rupees wasn't worth as much to me as it was to the boy, but it meant more to me after living in India for three years than it had when I'd first arrived. I'd grown accustomed to the culture's customs, straying from my lavish American ways and growing miserly. I resented paying more for housing, entrance to national monuments, food, and transportation because I was foreign.

Everyone in the crowd except one man encouraged the boy to take the 150 rupees I'd not yet offered. I didn't know what to do. I was certain, however, of some things: the boy would never see a doctor, his bicycle wheel would be pounded back into shape for a few rupees, the police would never come, and I'd ride away and never return. But I also knew I'd fail the boy no matter how much I gave him and, in turn, fail myself too.

I glanced at Chetan who stared nefariously at the crowd as I extracted a wad of rupees from my wallet and handed it to the boy, knowing it would never be enough. He unfurled his small hand and allowed me to put the money into his palm.

39

The Prize

Someone kickstarted Kali for me while several others helped me onto her. My right knee, my kickstart leg, bulged inside my split jeans, courtesy of the good doctor. The only parts of the leg that moved were my ankle and hip joint, but it was enough for me to ride. Chetan sat on his Kawasaki, gunning the engine impatiently. I'd decided to go to his home, as he promised it was "not far." I shifted Kali into gear with my right foot, thankful that my ankle worked, and eased out the clutch. Her tappets clacked and a faint grinding came from the front wheel as I followed Chetan away from the village. I hoped I wasn't damaging her. We hadn't ridden more than ten minutes when Chetan pulled to the side and jumped off his motorbike. "Just two minutes," he said over his shoulder as he trotted toward a house.

I balanced Kali with my good leg, questioning my decision to go with him and wishing he'd hurry up as stinging pain radiated from my kneecap. Overheating in all my gear again, nausea waved over me as I watched Chetan talk to a woman wearing a moo-moo and point back at me. He bobbled his head while the woman stared unimpressed at me before disappearing into the house. He returned a few minutes later waving my canteen—I hadn't realized he'd taken it—and tied it to Kali's rack.

"My relative. She filled your water," he said. Someone had drunk it while I was at the doctor's office. "Villagers think everything foreigners have is better."

Underway again, Chetan rode at a snail's pace, presumably so he wouldn't lose me, but it only made riding harder—speed is stability on a motorcycle. Kali teetered and I goosed her to give Chetan a hint, but he refused to take it. I trailed along thinking about the things he promised at his home: television, air conditioning, private room, hoping we would arrive soon. A jolt of excitement pulsed in me when he pulled to the side of the road again.

"My land," he claimed, sweeping his arm toward a stand of young, fruitless trees, as I pulled up next to him. "One hundred acres!"

I stared at the houseless, patchy orchard and gritted my teeth, disappointment welling in me. I wedged my left foot into the sandy soil to keep from toppling over. Speechless by his insensitivity, I glanced protectively at my right knee and saw the doctor's gauze bloomed red like a Rorschach. Chetan's euphoric face released a fury in me. The fool needed to quit mucking around. My lungs blazed with each breath and my knee felt numb. I needed to rest and recover.

"I'm in a lot of pain. How much further to your home?" I said.

"Yes, yes. Not far," he retorted, shifting his bike into gear and setting off again.

The environment was a mix of flat land stippled with budding apple and pear trees, cleaved by chunks of scarred and stripped land, the results of abandoned mines. The road was blessedly smooth, but even a single pebble had the power to launch a hellfire of raw pain in my body, and crossing a rickety railway track was my own personal Hiroshima.

In my months of riding, I'd become adept at judging time by miles, but the pain muddled my mind and three minutes felt like thirty, so I had no idea how long we rode. When Chetan stopped for the third time, a wave of rage roiled through me as he pulled into a *dhaba* filled with men, hopped off, and darted inside before I could stop him. I refused to shut Kali off and sat on her purring engine muttering in the blazing sun. Unable to dismount Kali without help and unsure of my ability to get back on as the soreness and stiffness intensified, I implored every supreme being within earshot, "Please, don't let him be long."

The three-sided *dhaba* looked more like a manger than a cafe. Hunched over a scattering of long benches and tables were truckers scooping curry with chapatis. Chetan stood in the opening waving frantically at me to join him. I shook my head, my brain felt sloshy, and shouted into a wall of heat, "I can't get off the motorcycle."

"Come. Come. I ordered you a coffee," he shouted, as he hustled toward me. "I will help you."

Drained from the events, I wavered but knew it was pointless to fight his need to parade me like a prized pig.

"Come. Come," he said, sounding irritated. "I am holding the motorcycle."

Easier to acquiesce, I slid off and hobbled after him. A cup of chai, not coffee, in a cracked cup with a missing handle, was plopped before me as I eked myself onto the bench. At least the sugar would revitalize me, I thought, blowing on the hot tea. Chetan swigged his and announced, "Chalo."

"But I'm not finished."

"Oh. Sorry. Okay," he said halfheartedly, then turned to the two grizzled men sitting across from us and regaled them with the day's events, ending with, "My entire program is ruined."

40

Breakdown

Chetan rode through his village to his house as if leading a ticker-tape parade. He parked outside a mammoth construction, at the end of a sunbaked road, set behind a crumbling compound wall. Seeing it, I realized the mournful building housed dozens of poor families. I tried to mask my disappointment as his promises of luxury slipped away, while he helped me off Kali and I heaved her onto her center stand. Neighbors' heads popped over balconies, rooftops, and doorways as Chetan escorted me through a rusty Gothic gate and into a mossy courtyard strangled with ancient vines. An old woman sprawled on a charpoy under a magnolia, her long gray hair hanging loose off the end like cobwebs, lifted her head quizzically and examined me with tenebrous eyes, questioning the logic of my appearance.

A younger woman came to the doorway of one of the ground-floor apartments. I thought she was Chetan's wife, but he led me past her without acknowledgment, heading toward a stone staircase in the corner of the courtyard. The place smelled like a barn and as I neared the stairs I saw the source of the scent: a water buffalo and her calf were curled at the foot of the stairs.

The cow rolled flat eyes over me, her mouth frothy with green and yellow juices from the dried grasses she munched. I feared they'd startle and jump up, but they remained blasé.

The stair treads were small and crumbling; my boots hung half off, making the ascent harrowing. I hauled my body up the flight by bracing my hands along the walls to prevent falling backward. Chetan's home roosted at the top, and as I reached it I saw through the open door a young man and boy sitting on a bed in a delightfully breezy and charming light-filled room. Alarmed by my arrival, they slid off the bed. Chetan introduced them as Aarav, his twenty-year-old son who attended college in Nellor, and Ram, his nephew who looked about twelve. The boys smiled stiffly and a woman Chetan said was his wife, Sita, leaned in from an adjoining room. She studied me but did not smile or speak.

"Sit. Sit," Chetan ordered, gesturing toward the bed.

It seemed too intimate, so I peg-legged to a chair next to it while Chetan launched into his well-worn story. I suspected it grew greater with each retelling, but the last line about his "program being ruined" never altered. When he'd finished, Sita smiled uneasily at me as she squatted in the doorway between the home's two rooms.

I looked around the happy room simply furnished with a full-size mattress on an iron bedstead, a cupboard, a ceiling fan, and a radio the boys were listening to when I arrived. Sita sat in the kitchen doorway. The home had no air conditioning, no television, and no privacy—unless they all intended to sleep in the kitchen while I occupied the bed. They had electricity but no private bathroom. The family shared the squat toilet at the foot of the staircase with everyone in the compound. I craved the restorative powers of a hot shower but knew it was out of the question.

Sita brought me a glass of water while Aarav fetched my bags and Ram scurried out to buy me a cold drink. When Aarav returned with my bags, I retrieved my first aid kit and took two aspirin before digging out my lungi to change into. The curtained kitchen was the only place that offered any privacy and I staggered into it to strip off my jeans, so I could clean the embedded gravel and dirt from my wound. Sita pulled a curtain behind me, but I heard them whispering as I propped myself against the counter and wiggled out of my pants. The tugging and twisting of undressing caused the frail scab covering the wound to crack and it started to bleed again.

Beyond the curtain, the room fell silent and I increased my effort to extract myself from the jeans, terrified one of them would burst in on me. The lungi wasn't ideal for wearing in front of these strangers, but my shell-shocked brain never considered the cargo pants that zippered off.

Naked and exposed, the urge to pee struck. I didn't want to climb down those stairs in such revealing attire or use that foul-smelling toilet, but I had no choice.

The family watched me solemnly as I appeared from the kitchen and asked "Toilet?" as I rummaged in my bags for a roll of toilet paper I carried, eager to avoid the cup and water the privy surely offered. Chetan snapped at Aarav to help me down the stairs. Inside the stall was worse than I'd imagined, but it became a real nightmare when I discovered I'd started my period. *Why me?* I groaned. My tampons and pads were tucked away in my saddlebags at the top of the stairs, and I wasn't capable of another trip up and down, so I stuffed wads of paper into my panties and hoped it was enough.

Lumbering back to the room, I saw Ram had reappeared with a Thumb's Up cola and a single cigarette. I hadn't smoked since my father and I gave it up together a year or so before he died. Quitting hadn't stuck for him; he'd been smoking since he was four, crawling under the house with his dad's discarded butts—a wild boy who thought he lived on a ranch, unaware they were tenant farmers. Ram tentatively handed them to me as if they were offerings he'd bring to a temple, then retracted to join the others huddled at the opposite end of the room. The distance between us made me feel on stage and keenly aware of the precarious arrangement of my loose attire. The loincloth provided little modesty.

I draped it to expose only my knee, tucking it tightly around my garishly white thighs so I wouldn't flash the family. Praying it all stayed in place, I peeled off the gauze covering the wound. Black and gray comet tails spiraled from the fleshy crater. The edges of the volcano-like hole were ragged and ruby while the center black, bloody, and engrained with grit. A point in the middle oozed pink. The family gasped at the injury. I held my breath to counter the wooziness. I wasn't equipped to handle this treacly lesion and cursed the doctor again for his incompetence.

Sita handed me a bottle of hydrogen peroxide and some cotton balls she pulled from a cupboard. As I timidly dabbed the wound, tufts of cotton clung to the dried blood. Lightheaded, I paused, waiting for the sick feeling to pass. I'm not the nursing type, but I don't pass out at the sight of blood. I'm like my mother, knowing I was the one the job fell to. But I didn't have the fortitude to pick the dirt and rocks out of my skin. I'd need to prime the wound by softening the blood so I could pry the gunk out. I poured a little stream of hydrogen peroxide onto the pulpy mess, watching it bubble satisfactorily.

"You are wasting the medicine," Chetan admonished, rising slightly from his seat. "Do it like this." He made a dabbing motion in the air.

I didn't think dabbing would work, but didn't want to upset him or have him yell at me, so I soaked a cotton ball with hydrogen peroxide and set it in the crater to soak. Chetan eyed me and the bottle suspiciously, still concerned about the amount I'd wasted. The soaked cotton worked to some degree, but it was painful and slow going. I could only do a little at a time, and kept stopping to wait for the waves of nausea to subside.

Sita smiled warmly at me as I picked pebbles from my skin in horror. Her initial skepticism morphing into motherliness and she insisted I take a break and rest in the bed. She wanted to feed me and dispatched Ram and Aarav to buy eggs and bread. I'd last eaten before the crash, around 9:30 a.m., and it was now almost 4:30 p.m.

Alone in the room with Chetan, I carefully stretched out along the edge of the bed while he reclined across the foot of it. We were silent as I breathed slowly and painfully, still concerned I'd cracked a rib or two.

"My house is dry," he said, in a guttural tone.

At first, I thought he meant alcohol, that if I wanted a drink to settle the trauma he couldn't oblige me. I started to say I didn't drink but before I had a chance, he continued.

"My purse is dry. My pockets are dry. We have no money."

Ah, I thought, he wants me to pay him for helping, for ruining his program.

He remained silent for a long time—the puttering of Sita in the kitchen and the sputtering of engines from passing vehicles the only sounds in the room—then he repeated his mantras of "ruined program" adding a verse on "dry pockets."

I couldn't handle another money talk, so I remained silent while he continued to financially probe me.

The boys returned, bursting into the room with supplies they delivered to Sita, before joining Chetan and me. With them in the room, Chetan's confessions ceased but resurfaced each time we were alone. Aarav asked me how many pieces of toast I wanted and I said one, but Sita returned with a mountain of scrambled eggs and four slices of toast—food and care to make me whole again.

"Thank you," I said, grateful for the food I needed to restore energy to my trembling limbs, but knew my stomach wouldn't let me eat it all.

41

Their Eyes Upon Me

Since arriving at Chetan's home, the sun passed over the house and with it the room's vibe changed from bright to disturbing as my shock gave way to realizing how lucky I was to be alive. I walked away from an accident I had no memory of, knowing one slight change in the scenario could have radically altered the outcome. I'd escaped death, paralyzation, broken bones, and ruptured organs. I rose from the highway and climbed back onto Kali and rode to this family's home. Now, I had to get out of there. Intellectually, I understood the danger of being alone with a concussion, but emotionally, I needed the solitude to heal. All I wanted was to curl up alone somewhere and process what happened, nursing myself whole out of sight of concerned eyes and far away from Chetan's shakedown.

My hand trembled as I lifted a spoonful of eggs to my mouth. My throat tightened, emotions coursing through me. *Don't cry. Don't cry. Don't cry*, I scolded myself. *You are NOT a crier.*

I cried. Tears trickled down my face for the first time since crashing.

Sita fretted. Her hands fluttered at the sight of my tears; her brown eyes welled as she glanced between her family and me.

"Please stop crying," Aarav said. "My mother is getting upset. She does not want you to be sad."

"I should go to a hotel," I said. "I appreciate everything you've done for me, but I'm in the way here."

"No! You must stay with us," he said. The alarm in his voice made me wonder if they felt responsible for my wellbeing since they took me in.

Sita crumpled her dupatta in her hands and tears pooled in her eyes as Aarav told her I wanted to leave. I didn't think she'd wanted me there when I'd arrived, now she didn't want me to leave. I hoped she wouldn't think she'd done something that made me want to go.

Chetan sat in the corner looking sour and grumbling it was a "bad idea." It might have been a bad idea physically but mentally it was vital.

"Please tell your mother I appreciate her kindness," I said to Aarav, "but I don't want to be a burden to your family."

Aarav continued to prevail I stay. Chetan didn't try to get me to stay, only groused the occasional "bad idea." I was grateful for his relative absence in the exchange, but he rallied once I convinced them my leaving had nothing to do with their care.

"I know an excellent hotel in Nellore," he said. "They know me there. It is an international hotel. It has an underground car park."

I remembered seeing Nellore on the map, it seemed a sizable town and likely offered many accommodations. If Chetan's choice of hotel turned out bad, at least I wouldn't hurt anyone's feelings by not staying.

"Aarav will ride your Bullet and you will ride on the back of my motorbike," Chetan announced.

"Papa, I have never driven a Bullet," Aarav said nervously.

"No matter. You drive it. You drive my motorbike. It is the same."

Aarav looked doubtful, knowing it wasn't the same. The Bullet was much heavier. Besides, I didn't want Aarav or anyone but me riding Kali. I explained to Chetan the differences between a Bullet and his little bike, but he shook his head saying, "Does not matter. He will learn."

"No, I rode the motorcycle here. I can ride it to Nellore." I wasn't as confident of this as I sounded. Riding required quick responses, especially in the city traffic I'd likely find in Nellore. Plus, it would be dark by the time we were on the road.

"He will do it," Chetan contended.

I looked at Aarav, slim with neat almost feminine mannerisms, and knew he would not learn to ride a Bullet today. I didn't want any more injuries, not for Aarav or Kali.

"I'll ride the Bullet," I said. "The highway is no place for a riding lesson."

Aarav looked relieved and Chetan, hearing the steel in my voice, relented. My body moaned as I stood and shuffled into the kitchen to change back into my jeans, then repacked my saddlebag. Aarav hauled it down the stairs and past the buffalos while Sita hugged me tightly as we said good-bye. I limped down the steep stairs as Chetan chattered about the hotel as the one his "Japanese clients" stayed in when they arrived on business. The idea of a hotel catering to foreign businesspeople sounded luxurious, and I imagined high-end services and a decadent bed.

"It is very expensive," Chetan boasted.

Leaving the home, I drew looks from the same neighbors who'd watched my arrival. Aarav kickstarted Kali and held her steady while I lifted my leg over the saddle. Out on the dark highway, Chetan didn't drive slowly this time, but sped ahead with

Aarav as I struggled to keep up. Traffic zipped past and I lost track of Chetan's taillight as he wove in and out of a slurry of vehicles. The crash stripped me of my confidence and I refused to jostle between cars and trucks as he did. Swallowed by darkness and traffic, I dropped further behind. Scooters and buses surged around me as I dodged people crossing the road, ghostly figures in a flood of one-eyed monsters. I slowed to avoid hitting someone and heard a clatter of metal on the road and knew Kali's toolbox had fallen open again. I pulled over and gingerly twisted around to see a trail of shiny silver wrenches winking on the road.

Chetan and Aarav were far ahead of me, and I couldn't dismount and remount Kali to retrieve them. Contemplating what to do, I saw the dark figure of a man bobbing in the dark like a chicken pecking for corn, picking up the tools. He trotted toward me with them and I thanked him. I was relocking the toolbox when Chetan and Aarav wheeled up next to me.

"Why are you sitting here?" Chetan shouted, over the road noise.

I saw no point in explaining it to him. When I didn't respond, he shot me an exasperated expression and said, "Try to keep up."

42

Redemption

The three of us stood in the dim, faux-gold lobby while Chetan handled my check-in, occasionally calling over his shoulder at me to confirm "Private bath, okay?" or "Single room, yes?" He barely waited for my replies, since my input was immaterial. As promised, the motel, not a hotel, had an underground parking garage for Kali, but little else lived up to his extolments.

Two boys carried my bags to the second floor and down a narrow outer passageway to my room, as Chetan, Aarav, and I followed like mountaineers led by sherpas. Inside, a full-size bed, two tired chairs, and a blemished coffee table consumed most of the little room. A desert cooler wedged into the window roared like a 747 jet, spewing semi-cool air into the muggy room that smelled of mildew and other unpleasantries. Mounted high on a wall at the foot of the bed hung a television; the hospital-like set up of it seemed appropriate.

"Cable TV," Chetan said, "and toilet." He pointed to a door a few feet from the bed that emitted smells of disinfectant and inefficient plumbing.

"*Thik hai. Thik hai.* Everything is *thik hai?*" he asked, eager for praise.

I nodded, grateful for the help and impatient for all of them to leave; a chorus of *get out* trilling in my head. The room looked and felt ashen and bleak with its lumpy, saggy bed and smelly bathroom packed into an eight-by-eight foot space. It was a dump, but it was my dump, with a locking door, anonymity, and above all privacy.

My knee throbbed and breathing still hurt. I'd decided my ribs were bruised and not broken. Tomorrow I'd find a competent physician for me and a mechanic for Kali. For now, I needed more pain reliever and sleep.

काली

Chetan pounded on the door at 9 a.m. the next day.

"Hello? Hello? Konie? Door is locked," he shouted. "Let me in."

I hadn't slept well and was awake but dozing, and yelled, "Just a minute."

Hot-poker pains stabbed my chest as I pushed myself upright, forcing me to pause and pant. I'd tended the wound with hydrogen peroxide (a bottle Aarav purchased the night before) before crawling into bed, leaving the bandage loose to allow air in. I slept half under and half out of the scratchy sheets, with my right leg exposed. Now, peeling back the gauze, I discovered the flesh around the opening was crimson and warm, while the gash teamed with greenish pus. It looked septic and made me queasy, so I covered it back up and waited for the sick feeling to pass.

"Door is still locked," Chetan bellowed, rattling the knob. "Open door."

I dressed and let him in, leaving the door open for the sake of propriety while he was in the room. He settled into one of the chairs, subdued for a long time, then picked up the phone and ordered chai. The same boy who'd delivered chow mein and a warm cola the night before returned with a tray of tea. He skirted my out-stretched leg and put the tray on the coffee table between the chairs. I asked the boy to get me some buttered toast and he briefly nodded before swiftly exiting the room. Chetan, sullen and silent, stroked his stubbled beard, his face darkening in contemplation. I drank the chai, deep in my thoughts of finding a doctor.

"I have no money," he said, cracking the quiet. "My business is no longer. Forty *lakh* in profits gone."

I tensed as his soliloquy continued.

"My pockets are dry," he whispered.

I grimaced then saw Aarav standing in the doorway looking solemn and anxious. He said he was on his way to college. If he was surprised to see his father sitting there, he didn't show it. Chetan said nothing to his son and no more about money, only stared at the floor while holding his cup near his face.

"How are you today," Aarav said, nodding toward my leg as he entered the room.

"Better, I think," although that wasn't true. The inflamed skin worried me. Was it blood poisoning? I asked Aarav about a doctor.

"Nellore is having many doctors," he said. "You will find them everywhere."

The boy returned with my toast and Aarav stepped aside to let him in. I ate while father and son observed. After a while, Chetan said something to Aarav I couldn't understand but wondered if it had to do with money or sex because Aarav's face flushed.

"I have to go to class. Is there anything I can do for you before I go?" he asked.

Chetan glowered at his son under his heavy, hooded eyelids for intruding.

"I need some more supplies from a chemist, and someone to fix the zipper on this little pack."

"My father can help you. I will return after class to do what I can," Aarav said, smiling wanly at me and avoiding his father's frostiness.

After Aarav left, Chetan ordered me to hurry up and eat so we could take care of my needs. On the streets, he hustled me in and out of shops and down alleyways, hunting for a sewing wallah, policing my moves with edicts of "Come here. Go there. Move aside. Hurry up." There was no getting away from him and I needed to rest, so I suggested lunch, asking him to choose the restaurant. That pleased him and he led me to a place kitty-corner from the hotel with a boisterous lunch clientele, where we were seated next to a family with a truculent child.

"Pico is very hungry," the mother exclaimed to the waiter, as she smoothed the boy's shiny black hair.

The boy—eight or nine—too old for public fits, pouted like a pompous little prince demanding food as the scrawny waiter scribbled the family's order.

"Better do as he wants," the father interjected, chuckling as he patted the boy's plump cheeks.

It was a wonderful distraction from Chetan's anthem. Unable to talk in the noisy restaurant, he devoured plates of butter chicken, *palak paneer*, saffron rice, *dahl*, *aloo gobi*, and *naan*, he'd ordered for us while I picked at the overly rich foods.

Chetan protested when I paid the waiter, and I wondered if doing so stripped him of his manhood. After lunch, I returned to my hotel room and he said goodbye, retreating like a general to reassess his combat strategy. I hoped I'd never see him again but knew that wasn't likely. He'd be back. His exhaustive and oppressive insinuations for money made me determined not to give him a single rupee.

काली

The doctor's office was two blocks from my hotel. His light-infused, plant-filled examining room felt healing compared to the crash-site doctor's office. Dr. Rosaiah—tall, slim, and in his sixties —introduced himself, shook my hand, and listened to my story of the accident and consequential treatment. I wore my zip-off pants this time so he could examine my knee.

Dr. Rosaiah washed and sterilized his hands with soap and alcohol, then prepped a tray of instruments. He instructed his nurse to remove the bandage from my wound, eyeing the red crater scrupulously before gently wiggling my kneecap. He cleaned it and sprayed an antibiotic sealer over the puncture, then wrote a prescription for antibiotics and pain, telling me to pick up B-complex as well. I hadn't trusted the other doctor enough to fill the prescription he'd written, but Dr. Rosaiah's humble mannerisms and reassuring smiles comforted me, reminding me of kindly doctors on television.

The doctor didn't believe I needed the knee X-rayed, saying he suspected nerve and ligament damage only, and assured me my body would heal on its own given time. He told me to leave the bandage off whenever possible to allow the air to generate scabbing. Otherwise, I was to keep the wound clean, stay off my leg as much as possible, take the pain pills as needed, and under no circumstances ride my motorcycle. "You must rest and heal," he said.

I did as instructed for the next few days, but the wound remained red and tender, throbbing as virescent pus seeped out. I returned to Dr. Rosaiah a couple of more times for him to clean and spray the wound with the sealer. "The colors are the body's way of purging itself of infection and impurities," he said. "Give it time, it will heal."

I didn't have time; Kali Puja was sixteen days and 991 miles away. Disobeying Dr. Rosaiah's instructions, I rode Kali to a mechanic recommended by the hotel clerk. Her front forks looked wonky and felt out of alignment. The mechanic, a cousin-brother of the clerk, pounded on Kali, conjuring up Nanna's warning about reckless mechanics who did more harm than good. I instructed the mechanic on how and what to do, which irritated him but gave me peace of mind.

Chetan and Aarav kept showing up. I was grateful for their concern, even if Chetan did continue to push his agenda. On their second visit, I told them I was well enough to travel—even though Dr. Rosaiah told me not to for at least ten days—and was leaving town.

Before the crash I rode between sixty-two miles and 234 miles a day, which took eight to fourteen hours, depending on road conditions. To arrive in Kolkata in time for Kali Puja I needed to ride at least sixty-two miles a day, no matter how long it took. In my state, however, I'd be lucky to ride five hours before the pain got too bad and I'd have to stop for the night.

Now that I was leaving town and would never see Chetan again, my iron-will to refuse his flagrant pandering softened. During my time alone with Chetan, I fervently ignored his less-than-subtle suggestions for compensation, but with Aarav in the room, I decided to bring up the subject and offered to pay the family for helping me. My words stung Aarav, and his complexion pinked with embarrassment at the proposal. "NO!" he cried, mortified. "It is our pleasure and duty to help you."

Chetan squirmed in his seat upon hearing this, vexation stewing in his dark eyes.

43

Making Time

Mounting and kickstarting Kali with an injured knee took skill and engineering. I couldn't bend or put much weight on my right leg, nor did it possess the sufficient force necessary to turn the engine over. The technique I'd once mastered of starting Kali on the first try was no longer a possibility. Instead of mounting and pumping the kickstart lever with my right leg just so, to allow the perfect mix of pressure and fuel to build in her chamber, instinctively sensing the apex of the process before kicking her to life with one swift thrust, I had to develop an alternative. Standing on the right side of Kali, I balanced on my mangled right leg and awkwardly plunged the lever down with my left leg. That leg—not attuned to the cadence of Kali—lacked force and precision, and she refused to start. After multiple tries, she'd eventually roar and I'd stagger around to the other side to lift my right leg over the saddle and place it on the footrest. The operation took five times longer than before the crash.

I surveyed my maps to see where I was and where I was headed. A long red line snaked up the eastern coast of India, a length equivalent to the distance between Florida and New York.

I searched it for cities large enough to offer decent hotels within sixty miles of each other, to plot my daily riding schedule to Kolkata. The highways on the East coast of India turned out to be in better condition than those up north. That part of the Subcontinent featured water canals and dense palm groves alongside grain fields. Farmers there spread harvested sorghum and millet stalks on canvases they laid onto the road for traffic to thresh for them. I didn't understand I was expected to ride over the grains and made wide berths around them. The farmers shouted at me and I thought it was because I hadn't skirted the cereals enough, so I went wider. But, they kept yelling. Finally, I saw cars and trucks plow over the crops and figured it out, but still rode skeptically over the pearly grains, disengaging the clutch to reduce the risk of losing traction.

I covered a miraculous 163 miles the first day, mainly because I didn't dismount for hours, but the progress came with a cost. Keeping my knee locked in a bend for so long resulted in it swelling and throbbing like a hot piston. I had to rest the next day and revise my riding schedule. I parceled the remaining thirteen days into a pattern of one day riding between 160 and 190 miles, followed by two to three laid up in a hotel nursing my knee.

Traffic steadily thickened the farther north I rode, as did the frequency of wrecked trucks rusting alongside the highway. Some days I counted twenty crashes. Boredom, the threat of another wreck, and my pounding knee intensified the looping song in my head about a bullfrog being a good friend of mine.

Ten days after the accident the skin around the puncture remained a raw septic hole with chartreuse discharge. I cleaned it nightly and left it uncovered while sleeping, only to discover the sickening goo had replenished. The crusty veil that formed overnight ripped open as soon as I bent my leg getting out of bed. I stopped taking the prescription pain pills when I left Nellore because I didn't want to be dopey on the bike, but I popped aspirin hourly for the pain. Even though Dr. Rosaiah didn't indicate a need for an X-ray, contending the injury would heal naturally, I grew doubtful and decided to find a hospital in Visakhapatnam.

Seven Hills Hospital looked down on a gray city constructed with gray buildings. The receptionist handed me a slip of paper with a number and a doctor's name on it before directing me to a window to pay in advance. I paid and joined a crowd of cheerless people in casts and bandages assembled in the waiting room. When it was my turn, the doctor's nurse ushered me to an examining room where the physician pressed around on the kneecap and ordered an X-ray.

The technician swiveled a gigantic green scanner that looked like an alien insect from a 1950s sci-fi film strategically around to capture images of my injury. Zip. Zap. Finished. I returned to the examining room and the doctor read the film placed on a large light-board attached to the wall.

"As I suspected, there is no fracture," he said. "I am going to show you how to wrap your leg with this elastic bandage. It will provide support and help reduce the swelling."

"What about the pus?" I asked, adding, "How long before the swelling goes away?"

"I suspect you do not take good care of yourself," he said, eyeing my scruffy appearance, "and as a result, your body is fighting the infection slowly. It will take ten days for the swelling to disappear completely. I suggest that you do not ride during that period. But ... I doubt if you will do that."

He was right. I had to be in Kolkata—550 miles north—in six days for Kali Puja.

The 214-mile ride along the Andrea Pradesh and Odisha border to Berhampur the next day took seven hours, with six of them (or so it felt) in bumper-to-bumper traffic among idling engines burping black soot. By the time I got to Berhampur— where European silk traders built their mansions—the light was fading and I almost missed the sign for town. My guidebook said the mansions were strung along the riverfront and I hoped one might offer lodging, but when I couldn't find either the river or the mansions I checked into a hotel that offered cable television. I discovered the *Wizard of Oz* was on that evening, and ate, showered, and tended my wound before propping my leg on a pillow ready for a night of nostalgia. I'd pushed myself hard since leaving Nellore to reach Kali Puja in time, but watching Dorothy battle flying monkeys and wicked witches to get home made me realize I too wanted to be home.

It was October—ninety-seven days and 4,970 miles since leaving New Delhi. It was more than days and miles that wore me down. The crash took something out of me, or perhaps put something in me. An understanding that being alone in the world didn't necessarily mean freedom. Like Dorothy, I missed my friends and family. I missed the sanctuary of home. I missed familiar faces and the comfort of a predictable routine. I was ready to go home. For me, home was in New Delhi—the last "home" I knew, where friends lived. I'd been away from the United States for so many years now that it felt foreign, and I had a hard time imagining myself there. But I wouldn't get back to New Delhi anytime soon. I'd begun my journey with the plan to ride along the edge of the Subcontinent, and I intended to finish what I started.

44

Dreams

My last city before reaching Kolkata was Khanagpur. The day started wrong and got worse—I banged my knee loading Kali, a gas station attendant insisted on "American dollars" instead of rupees, a chai wallah's dogs lunged at me growling and snarling, the road was a minefield of rubble, Kali's engine overheated in more stalled traffic, and she ran out of gas. The only upside to the day was when I ran out of gas, I was within coasting distance to an Indian Oil station. By the end of the day, I no longer sang about a bullfrog but had changed my tune to "Fuck India."

Checking into the hotel, I snarled at the clerk and nearly took the head off the young receptionist who served me a warm cola. Kali's forks leaked oil and I asked the clerk for directions to a mechanic. He gave me directions to his cousin's shop and I dumped my stuff before heading over. I found the mechanic grunting and shoving a new wheel onto the drum of an old scooter.

Singh wore his turban small, flat, and tight across his forehead—not high in a peak like the merchants of New Delhi—and said he couldn't get to Kali until 6 p.m. He reminded me of

Nanna somehow, so I trusted him. I returned to the hotel for a nap to sleep off my angst, hoping he wouldn't need to order a part—ensuring I'd miss Kali Puja. Irrationally I thought, *If I miss the festival the entire journey will be a waste.*

Singh and a customer were sitting on a small bench when I arrived precisely at 6 p.m. The twilight mauve sky drenched the place in peace, evoking the feel of an Edward Hopper painting.

The men smiled as I got off Kali.

"He said you, an America, would be punctual," said the man, nodding toward Singh. It was his scooter the mechanic was working on that afternoon, and it was still parked in the garage surrounded by a moat of tools.

The nap had worked and I smiled, wondering how many Americans passed through Singh's shop.

Mopping sweat from his brow and lifting his thick-lensed glasses to blot his eyes, the man introduced himself as Mr. Chatterjee, the English teacher at a nearby school. His sparse hair lay arranged in a deep comb-over—the part starting an inch above his right ear. I sat next to him on the wooden bench while Singh dispatched a young helper for chai. As the boy hurried off, he wheeled Mr. Chatterjee's scooter out of the garage and pushed Kali in.

"You are on an adventure?" Mr. Chatterjee asked.

I suspected he knew some of my story already, at least he knew by my license plate that I came from New Delhi. I filled in a general outline of my journey and he smiled, stretching his bushy mustache into a wide fringe across his face.

"I'm a traveler too, although I have not visited all the places you have. I always tell the school children they must travel," he said. "Please, madam, tell me all the countries you have visited."

I visualized a map of the world as I named the dozens of countries in the order I'd traveled.

"You must meet my children," he said. "Please come to my class tomorrow and tell them about your adventures."

I thought about it, but I knew I wouldn't. It was Tuesday night and Kali Puja was Thursday. Meeting his class meant risking missing the festival as I still had a hundred miles to ride. Too many things could derail my arrival.

"I'm sorry, but I can't," I said selfishly.

"The children could learn so much from you that I cannot teach them. Hearing about your adventures will stir their dreams," he said. "They must dream if they are to do anything in life."

"I have to get to Kolkata for the Kali Puja," I said. Abandoning my search for the other shakti peetha temples made me superstitious about missing it.

Mr. Chatterjee nodded silently, the moonlight glistening on the patches of his bald head peeking through hanks of hair.

"I'm really sorry, but I've traveled for months to be there on Kali Puja."

"Of course. I understand. It was just a thought."

The tea arrived and we sipped contemplatively for a few moments before Mr. Chatterjee spoke again, this time inquiring how much I paid for my hotel room, the cost of Kali, and life in America before rounding back to the subject of his students.

"Several years ago, one of my students won an international award for a short story he wrote," Mr. Chatterjee said wistfully. "He was an excellent writer and loved writing very much. He could have been a great author."

"What happened? Did he stop writing?"

"His family wanted him to be a doctor," he said shaking his head. "Our children have a lot of family pressures which causes their own dreams to fade."

We sat silently on the bench under the dense Milky Way, the sounds of Singh's tinkering with Kali just inside the garage. I thought about dreams, and what it means to dream. Did we ever attain them, or did our dreams merely battle life's realities? Could they be the same—dreams and realities—or was a dream a dream, and life something else? Wasn't I living my dream?

I outgrew wanting to be a cowboy (cowgirls didn't exist on television in the 1960s) in favor of being a paleontologist, traveling the globe digging up prehistoric dinosaur bones. But I'd still longed for a horse. When I was thirteen, my brother , who'd lobbied our parents for years, got one. Once he had his, it didn't take me long to get one too: a pretty little bay registered American Quarter Horse named Bert. We boarded our horses at a stable surrounded by wooded trails and swarming with kids our age who had their own horses. On Saturdays we mucked stalls and drank Big Red sodas before hitting the wooded trails, crossing a pig pasture owned by the farmer next door.

The pigs terrified me, especially the sows who nursed their piglets in a camper shell next to the gate we passed through to the woods. My brother and his friends teased me. "They'll eat you," they claimed when it was my turn to open the gate. They'd mastered opening the gate without dismounting, but I was smaller and had to lean so far over I was certain I'd fall and their warning would come true.

One of the farmer's old mares died and he'd buried her in a shallow grave in the pig pasture. For weeks, I watched the horse's bones slowly emerge as the pigs picked her clean, an idea formulating in the back of my mind. I decided to retrieve the bones and reconstruct the horse in my dad's garage, the way museums did when paleontologists discovered dinosaur bones.

Overriding my fear of the pigs and conjuring up courage, I managed to snag a jawbone and steal it home, hiding it in the garage, pushed far back on a ledge so my dad wouldn't find it. Next, I got a foreleg and tucked it alongside the jawbone. Before I could get more, my father found the bones and confronted me. His face displayed spectacular shades of purple as he fumed about the diseased bones, insisting the "filthy things" be tossed. Disappointed my paleontology career ended before it began, I always wondered what the garbage men thought of my family when they collected our trash and discovered horse bones.

45

Kali Puja

The goddess Kali's big right toe, symbolizing self-expression and joy, resided at the Kalighat Kali Temple. I flagged down an elderly taxi driver with rheumy eyes and a lively gray mustache to take me to the temple. He spun the cab's wheel as if steering an ocean-liner and deposited me at the gate, giving me the number of his cab so I could find him later. The streets around the temple bobbed with people on their way to pay homage to the goddess and entreat her blessings.

A clean-shaven man in a remarkably white kurta and salwar approached me as I neared the gate. He smiled and introduced himself as one of the temple priests and offered to show me around. I figured him for a hustler and not a priest, but removed my shoes and followed him into the courtyard anyway. My hot bare feet left steamy footprints on the courtyard stones that mingled with, and were lost among, the other pilgrims' prints. Worshippers carried flowers, incense, and fruit offerings for the Mother Goddess. Some wore grotty rag-like apparel while others were wrapped auspiciously in saffron and gold.

I'm apprehensive in temple crowds, having read too many news reports of devotees being trampled to death in inexplicable stampedes—but allowed myself to be nudged into the flow of people by my guide.

"This is the barren tree," he said, stopping at an old and twisted tree ensconced behind a marble wall with an iron grill. "It is the barren tree because women wishing to get pregnant tie tiny stones to it, hoping their stone will blossom into a bud on the tree."

The women pressing to get close to the tree were either hopefuls or gratefuls—women whose stone budded on the tree and they'd given birth, returning to thank the goddess for her blessed fertility.

"Take a photo," he encouraged. He didn't invite me to tie a pebble to the tree, and I wondered if he thought I was too old or foreigners weren't allowed. I was thirty-seven and had never desired children.

I snapped a shot to appease him, and he ushered me toward the sacrificial pen where hundreds of goats had already been slaughtered to honor the bloodthirsty goddess Kali. There weren't any goats in the pens, as most of the killing and butchering was done the previous day so the meat could be cooked and served to the poor on Kali Puja. I was grateful I wasn't subjected to the killings or hearing the bleats of terrified goats, seeing the blood-soaked tree stump with tufts of hair in the crevices was disturbing enough.

Hindus believe in reincarnation—a chance to be born into a better physical life over and over. More than one person had told me Indian servants were content to watch their bosses consume rich curries while they survived on plain rice and little protein, knowing their next life would be better if they appeased the gods and goddesses in this life. I don't believe in an afterlife, but like to think there's an energy that connects all beings—a kinetic fabric of humanity—that absorbs us when we die and allows our essence to live on after death.

At the end of the tour, the guide fluttered his small hands at a registration book, asking me to sign and give him my donation. There were more rooms and cubbies to see, but he didn't offer to take me and I wasn't interested. I'm unsure what I expected to happen at this shakti peetha temple, a transformation? To suddenly see myself with clarity after months of confusion? To have the goddess confirm some false idea I had of myself? Nothing happened. I walked out the gate the same person I'd been when I'd entered.

I wandered past tables packed with Kali kitsch. Pausing to inspect the images of the wild goddess on everything from posters to pendants, I searched for something to pay homage to the celebrations. None among the baubles spoke to me. I began my journey intending to find pieces of the goddess and making her whole again—a rebirthing of myself. Although I'd abandoned the plan early on, realizing it was a construct and not an enthusiasm, I imagined I'd feel something liberating at Kali Puja. Instead of feeling unfettered, I sensed the weighty hollowness of an emotional void—as if I'd lost part of myself along the way.

Full Circle

46

Crossing Over

The setting sun gave way to swarms of insects that splattered me in gooey blotches as I rode through them. I found their carcasses secreted away in crevices of my body when I arrived in Baharampur at the end of a ten-hour, 110-mile day.

The night pressed in as I rode down the wide empty main road, feeling like a cowpoke coming in from weeks on the range, looking for a hot bath and a clean bed. The town possessed a deserted air, but the few people out turned to look as they heard Kali's engine. Noticing I wasn't one of them, they pointed down the street and shouted, "Hotel," directing me to a place on the edge of a swamp, where the bugs reached blood-draining magnitudes.

When I lived in the United States, I'd had hoity-toity standards and refused to stay at prosaic chain hotels on the basis they were "icky" and "smelled funny." But after years of traveling on a budget, my standards drifted downward and I didn't balk at the condition of the room next to a swamp. It offered a stained narrow mattress on a cement slab, draped with a filthy mosquito net, and a private bath occupied by a colossal, glistening bullfrog, that observed me with pronounced displeasure when I opened the door. Jeremiah, no doubt. I apologized and closed the door.

On the way out of town the next morning, I passed a pristine new hotel—clean sheets, hot showers, and no frogs—before hooking onto National Highway 34. Spilling into countryside lusher than I imagined existed in India, I puttered between rolling pastures, swaying crops, and sparkling ponds. Ancient, leafy deciduous trees edged the road like palace guards, cooling the air and emitting earthy smells that transported me to my childhood days in Indiana.

With Kali Puja behind me, the urgency to push myself hard dissipated. New Delhi was within 1,200 miles—a week away if I rode hard and long days. But what would I be rushing to? I'd given up my apartment and gotten rid of or stored my things in boxes at Patralekha's home. I had no job. The road had become my way of life, and as hard as it was, I wavered—simultaneously reluctant for it to end and eager for it to be over. Like every new phase in life, the unknown was intimidating.

काली

I arrived in Raiganj—a dusty, ghostly town—around 2 p.m., and looped a chain through Kali's front tire and frame, padlocking the ends together and checked into a hotel. I still worried about people messing with her, but less so now. It'd been three weeks since the crash and my ribs had finally healed but the hole in my kneecap remained an angry pit, although the pus had subsided and a scab formed.

I wandered around the desolate town, the sun too blistering for sane folks to be out and about, feeling sticky and bored before returning to my room for a nap. I roused long enough for a late dinner and was stretched out on the bed, trying to get cool under a speeding ceiling fan, when someone pounded on the door. I staggered dully to it.

"Madam, come. Move motorcycle," said a young man, a mix of excitement and angst in his body language.

I followed him downstairs to where Kali was secured under the hotel's covered breezeway, between stores selling dry goods, cloth, and sweetmeats. Everything was shuttered except for a chai wallah's shop where an old proprietor stood patiently waiting. The shopkeeper insisted I put Kali into his place overnight for security, indicating trouble if I didn't. Once, I'd have been grateful and would have happily lugged Kali into the shop, but now I hesitated. It was a lot of bother to maneuver a 500-pound motorcycle up steps and into a tiny space.

The town bordered Bihar, India's most lawless state. Its reputation for crime dated back to the twelfth century, when assassins known as Thugs roamed 'the roads, robbing and strangling travelers with red *roomaals* in the name of the goddess Kali. The threat of highway robbery remained real, with India's modern-day robbers known as dacoits, and Bihar's reputation for them dominated the newspapers. The most famous female bandit was a former New Delhi neighbor, Phoolan Devi. We'd frequented the same beauty parlor.

Born poor in rural India, she was married off at eleven years old to a man three times her age who beat her. She escaped his brutality, but her family refused to take her back. Alone in the world, the only people who'd take her in was a gang of dacoits. She married the leader, and, after a rival gang murdered her husband and repeatedly raped Phoolan, she formed her own outlaw posse and became legendary as the Bandit Queen.

Phoolan, a pretty woman with a coquettish smile, robbed and killed villagers from 1979 to 1983 while wearing a red roomaal tied around her head (said to match her red lipstick and nails) and a bandolier across her chest. She was a hero to the poor and oppressed, but her undoing came on February 14, 1981, when her gang entered a village to rob it and Phoolan recognized the men as her husband's killers and her rapists. Sick with revenge, she dragged the men from their homes and executed them. She evaded the police for two years, but later surrendered and was sentenced to eleven years in prison. While locked away, she insisted she only robbed from the rich to give to the poor, especially poor women. Upon release, she became a politician and member of Lok Sabha, India's lower house of Parliament.

"Inside, madam," the teen said, as we stood outside the old man's chai shop. "Put inside."

"She won't fit," I said, seeing no room for her among the tightly packed chairs and tables.

"Yes, yes. Inside." He nodded and motioned his hands as if to urge me along.

Even if she fit, I couldn't push her up the three steps leading into the shop. The boy sensed my objections and hauled a splintery plank on top of the steps, calling two men over and indicating they push Kali inside. I relented and unchained her.

They heaved her over the stairs and settled her amongst the chairs and tables. The old man slammed the iron shutters down and clicked a thick padlock at the bottom.

The next morning, as the old man supervised, two boys rolled her out, telling me I owed ten rupees.

"But it was your idea," I protested, reaching for my wallet.

The old man and boys rewarded me with smiles as I handed the shopkeeper the cash.

काली

I turned west onto Highway 31 two hours later and crossed into Bihar. The coolness I enjoyed in West Bengal abruptly turned into dry heat, as the terrain shriveled from lush green to parched weeds, as I headed for Munger. According to my maps, the historic city was on the banks of the Ganges River, about 100 miles from Raiganj. But I misread the map and instead of a few hours ride it took nine, as I wasted time looking for a bridge that didn't exist.

Finally, I gave up and followed a dirt track toward what I hoped was a village. It led me to a field of weeds trampled down by old men carrying bundles wrapped in faded carpets on their heads, younger men toting camouflage-covered suitcases, and women and children bedraggling behind, all clearly headed somewhere. I puttered behind the procession, unable to see where they were going because of a little hill. Cresting it, I saw a string of jeeps parked pell-mell around a cluster of chai stalls on the banks of the Ganges. I rode to the chai stalls and asked a grizzled man in a dhoti about the bridge.

"No bridge," he said. "Boat."

The choppy gray water sparked with spiky waves in the mid-afternoon sun. The small skiffs pinned to the shore looked as if they'd carry six or seven people, but never a motorcycle.

"A boat?' I asked, as if inquiring would make a more suitable one appear.

"*Haanji,*" he confirmed. "Big boat."

I rescanned the river's horizon for a ferry, but only saw rowboats bouncing on the rough water like toys.

"You need boat?" asked a young man balancing a suitcase expertly on his head.

"Not one of those," I said. "They're too small."

"No. They are not," he insisted.

They appeared improbably risky for carrying people and not remotely suitable for conveying a motorcycle. Surely there was another way to Munger, I thought, and took out my map. There was a bridge, but my calculations were off by at least ninety miles. I'd not passed through any towns and was too tired to keep going, and decided to take my chances with a boat. I slipped Kali's front wheel over the dune toward the river's edge, thinking, *Munger better be worth it*, as Kali fishtailed on the sand.

I stopped some yards from the Ganges and gazed at a half a dozen dinghies rocking in the water. Women lifted their saris to clamber in, as men passed suitcases and bedrolls to the boat wallahs. Loaded with more passengers than was safe, the captains shoved off. If Kali fit in one, it would have to be between the seat planks, and then it would be tight.

A boatman ambled over to discuss price, but when I said no to his costly offer he leveled a disappointed stare and shuffled away. I started Kali's engine and turned to leave, deciding it wasn't worth the hassle or peril.

"Did he refuse?" asked the man I'd talked to up by the chai wallahs.

"No. We couldn't agree on a price."

"I am sorry," he said. "How much did he want?" His face scrunched up when I told him. "That is too much."

"How much should it cost?"

"Five rupees," he said. "Please, may I try for you?"

I knew a motorcycle and a foreign woman would cost more than five rupees, but less than the hundreds the boatman wanted to charge me. The man returned with several sinewy men in tow and saw my worry at the thought of them hoisting Kali into one of those boats.

"Do not worry, madam," he assured me. "That is not your concern."

But it was and I hovered after them, terrified they'd drop her in the river.

The men dragged the dinghy up onto the shore, grabbed different sections of Kali's frame, lifted her—gear and all—and tottered toward the boat. They splashed through the water and attempted to put her front wheel over the port side, but the boat glided away and I held my breath. The four men frantically shouted at the men holding the boat, who shouted back. Finally, they managed to shove Kali into the boat, wedging her front and rear tires between starboard and port. I clambered in after her, along with Ashok, my negotiator, and four other passengers— plus, two oar men, a boy to collect the money, a pole man, and the captain.

"Can you swim?" Ashok joked.

I calculated the risk of sinking in my head, estimating our boat's weight based on what I saw in the other skiffs. If captains routinely packed in thirty people who weighed an average of what looked about ninety pounds each, then most boats managed to carry a load of 2,700 pounds. There were nine men, one boy, me, and a motorcycle in ours. Kali weighed 500 pounds, while the rest of us brought the weight up to roughly 1,400. Far less than what the boats probably shuttled. Still, there were no guarantees. What if the boat sprung a leak halfway across the river? What if the weight shifted and we capsized? I could dog paddle but Kali would sink to the bottom and be lost forever.

The men poled and rowed the boat across strong turgid currents that skewed the boat's direction, despite the men's efforts. Halfway across the spirited river, the boy collected the fares and I handed him 100 rupees. His eyes darted to the captain but he didn't react, only watched the shore. Ashok chatted, telling me he was a law student at the university in Munger and crossed the river three or four times a week, but he didn't tell me the fee he negotiated. I couldn't read the boy's expression and didn't know how much he expected. Money's a tricky subject, coupled with culture made it more confusing for me. I turned away and scanned the shore, hoping we'd work it out on land.

"Where will the boat dock?" I asked Ashok.

"Do not worry, madam, that is not your concern," he said, his mantra for worried women.

But I was worried. As we neared the shore, I saw a thin strip of beach and a zigzag trail up a steep incline to the road. I'd never ridden Kali off road and wasn't confident about doing so for the first time on a steep sandy dune.

When we beached, Kali proved more difficult getting out of the boat than going in, but the men managed to deliver her unscathed to dry land.

"Okay, madam," Ashok said. "You drive up there."

The track appeared even more dangerous up close. Not a path but a rut scored into a dramatically steep hill.

"I can't. She's not a dirt bike."

The men looked at each other for a moment then tugged Kali to the top, where a discussion broke out among the crew and Ashok. I thought it was about money. Thought they wanted more for carrying Kali up the hill.

"Fifty rupees," Ashok said, and I reached for my wallet, but he stopped me. "No. He owes you fifty rupees. You gave 100 and his charge was fifty rupees only, but he has no change and cannot repay you."

"I don't want any change," I said.

"This is from your good side," Ashok said.

His remark surprised and embarrassed me, since my good side wasn't something I'd experienced much of lately. Earlier I'd thought the boy was angling for more money. My experiences with people and money—not just in India but Egypt, Jordan, Syria—had conditioned me to think the subject of money always had many chapters. It was almost never straightforward, yet I continued to want it to be and acted as if it were while knowing it wasn't.

47

Mi Amore

A breeze blew across the ashram's compound as I sat in the shade of the dining hall sipping tea from a small bowl and thinking about nothing. I'd arrived in Bodh Gaya, the birthplace of Buddhism, five days earlier lured by its claim in my guidebook of it being an "oasis from the dust and noise" of India. The grounds were designed to elicit harmony, with guest rooms, immaculate and containing a cot and desk, overlooking the compound's bright beds of flowers and meditation *gompa*. Monks and long-term Buddhist practitioners, seeking higher levels of enlightenment, slept in rudimentary huts at the back of the property.

I'd never practiced meditation before, but the idea appealed to me after four months on the road. Buddhism could teach me to let go and not form attachments to ideas, events, and people. It could teach me that things were things and thoughts were thoughts, and I didn't need to control everything.

I enrolled in a three-day silent meditation course that prohibited all forms of communication, including eye contact. As an American, I always make eye contact, despite it being a cultural no-no in some countries. It's seen as an invitation by males and had brought me unwanted attention many times, but it's hard to break ingrained ways.

My knee was mostly healed, but sitting in the lotus position, legs lapped over each other like a pretzel, rejuvenated the pain, and sent shooting stabs through me. I struggled physically to "sit through the pain" as instructed, but the soreness of sitting like a sadhu didn't compare to the jitters stillness brought, what Buddhists call the monkey mind.

On the third and final day of the retreat, I sat in the dining hall resting between one of six daily meditations, gazing across the compound, when I heard the unmistakable thumping of a Bullet. Looking was a no-no, but the Bullet's throaty rumble roused my interest, and I peeked to see a man getting off the motorcycle. He parked his battle-scarred bike—a beefy 500cc with a wide grinning crash guard across its face—next to Kali. He was in his early forties and dusty from the road. I saw tenderness in his cocoa eyes and a warm grace in his face. I stared, unable to tear my eyes away. The rational part of me knew my feeling was not real but rather what the Buddha had called an attachment, the very thing that would lead to suffering. But it didn't feel like suffering, it felt like love—and I didn't even know his name.

I broke eye contact, chastised myself for falling off the wagon, and wandered over to the gompa for a meditation tuneup session, putting as much distance between me and the gorgeous stranger as possible. Walking across the grassy lawn, inhaling the fragrances of jasmine and frangipani, a thought occurred to me: This was the last day of my silent retreat. After midnight, I was free to pursue my feelings for the Bullet wallah.

काली

I learned the golden-skinned stranger was an Italian named Antonio—an ex-monk who once traveled with the Dalai Lama around the world, as part of his entourage. After twenty years of devotion, Antonio wanted to experience other things in life. When I heard that, my conviction, that we were meant to be together, deepened. We had so much in common, not only the motorcycle connection but we were both in search of some kind of freedom.

Every day, I lingered in the garden or dining hall, hoping Antonio would seek me out and pick up where our eyes had left off. When he didn't, I rationed it away: *People would talk if we were together constantly. His restraint showed respect for the Center, a place where sex was forbidden.* Even though our conversations remained platonic, I sensed his feelings for me each time I caught him stealing glances at me.

One day we took a ride together on our Bullets, stopping along the Ganges River. Gazing over the rippling murky water, I hoped Antonio would kiss me and willed it to happen. But it didn't. Instead, he talked about motorcycles, road conditions, and the places we'd both visited. I consoled myself with the fact he'd spent decades in a monastery. He needed to take it slow, and I was happy simply being near him.

Since kisses weren't coming soon, I distracted myself by devoting time to Kali. I pulled her spark plug and sat in the magnolia's shade scraping off carbon buildup with my knife, practicing mindfulness as thoughts of Antonio danced at the edge of my consciousness. I checked her tappets after cleaning the plug; they rolled free under my thumb so I moved onto the gas filter, washing and drying its tiny screen. I topped off her oil and added some to the front forks as well, since they still leaked from the crash. Her chain was a bit slack, so I tightened it. When

I finished with all the adjustments, I found a bucket and sponge, giving her the well-deserved pampering she'd not had since the Saraswati festival in Mamallapuram.

Gleaming again, I tried to start her up but she wouldn't turn over. Antonio was sitting on a bench nearby and heard the misfire.

"Air. Air," he shouted.

I should have been embarrassed by the obvious oversight, but as I pulled the choke I absurdly thought, "He cares. He's looking out for me." I felt like a lovesick fourteen year old as I fantasized what it would be like when we were together. What his kisses would taste like? Where we would go after leaving the ashram? Would we remain in India? Perhaps we'd live in New Delhi or ride to Dharamsala to be near the Dalai Lama, once we were married. Maybe he would want me to return to Italy to live, or perhaps we'd go to the United States.

Despite the joy these escapist's thoughts brought me, a niggling voice in my head insisted I was really suffering. My love for Antonio was a fleeting attachment that would result in sorrow when the reality did not live up to the dream. At night I wrestled with the voice while my monkey mind bounced around, and wondered if Antonio was thinking about me.

Knowing I needed to purge all thoughts of Antonio, I signed up for a second retreat, this one a six-day silent course. But when the fantasies ceased to diminish, I asked Kansho, a Frenchman who gave up his secular life to become a monk, how monks dealt with sexual desires.

"We meditate on the decaying flesh of the one we desire," he said. "First, the skin turns black, swells, puckers, and shrivels. As the flesh rots and falls off, we observe the bones becoming brittle. We imagine…."

I couldn't bring myself to have those ugly thoughts about Antonio's body, and let my mind ruminate down beautiful carnal avenues instead.

काली

"Something has happened to you since you've come here," said Donna, who, along with her husband Tom, were the ashram's directors. We were waiting in line for lunch one day after my second dose of enlightenment training.

"What do you mean?"

"You've changed. You look absolutely bloomy. Have you fallen in love?"

I shook my head no, afraid my voice would give me away.

Meditation hadn't cleared Antonio from my mind, so I decided to join a few others for dinner at a little restaurant in town. I hadn't ridden Kali in days and decided to ride her, rather than walk the half mile with the others. As the light faded over plowed fields, I saw two people stop and talk to someone on a scooter. Riding the gravel road toward them, I saw it was a police officer.

"The cop says there are reports of bandits in the area and we should turn back," Jim, a guy from my second round of enlightenment, said to me.

The police officer, who hadn't paid attention to me before, turned to peer closely at me. I wore my helmet but not the dupatta over my face.

"You ride this Bullet, madam?" he asked dubiously.

The words, "I'm riding it, aren't I," bubbled up but I didn't let them out, only nodded.

"Go," he said, shooing me. "You will have no trouble."

Vivian and Jim decided to turn back, dust puffing in their wake as they tromped to the compound, but I continued on since several others were already at the cafe.

Mark, Tammy, and Beth had a steamy platter of dumplings before them when I arrived at the Tibetan restaurant. Collections of monks and raggedy travelers were hunkered over smoldering bowls of *thukpa*, as rickshaws and scooters buzzed past like angry flies, and Bollywood ballads blared from speakers, sounding more like mad cats than music. After days of silence, the clattering pots, hissing cauldrons, and rowdy patrons slurping down soup under glowing paper lanterns was intoxicating. We wolfed down spicy, succulent veg dumplings, their sizzling contents squirting into our mouths like sin.

"Did you hear there was going to be trouble?" Tammy asked.

"There was a cop on the road when I left," I said. "He said there were robbers in the area."

"Apparently, there has been a lot of trouble around here lately," she said. "I heard an Israeli guy got shot the other day."

"I heard he refused to give them his wallet when they surrounded the rickshaw he was in," Mark added.

"What was he thinking?" Beth said.

"If bandits demand my money, I'm giving it," I said. That wasn't entirely honest, since I doubted I'd hand over the contents of my money belt unless the robbers knew about it.

After we devoured the dumplings, I ordered a bowl of rice soup made from yak stock and seasoned with roots, while the others opted for thukpa. The waiter brought our main courses—along with a basket of charred and puckered flatbread from the wood-fueled oven—and our conversation turned to gossip, airing the scuttlebutt of who hooked up with whom after our meditation course. The practice of sexual repression stirred desires and drove people to act. But if anyone suspected the secret bond between Antonio and me, they didn't mention it.

We capped off the evening with mugs of coffee before heading back to the ashram. Rather than walk and risk being robbed, the group hired a rickshaw. I didn't want to wait while they negotiated a price and rode back alone. A bright moon lit the empty road as I rolled along, half enjoying the nip in the November air and half alert to danger.

At the ashram's gate, the old chowkidar rose from the stool he sat on snoozing with his back to the wall. Wrapped in a thin tartan blanket, he hobbled over and creaked open the gate, saluting me as I rode in. I parked and walked over to Donna sitting on a bench, blissfully ignoring the cloud of mosquitoes buzzing around her. In the dimness, pearls of sweat glistened on her arms and neck. I joined her and together we blew and flicked mosquitoes away, mindful of the precept to not kill any sentient being. I felt uncomfortable about the suggestion of robbers breaking into the compound. It seemed unusual for the police to send an officer to warn of trouble, and asked Donna about it.

"I wouldn't worry," she said. "There's lots of talk about bandits in the area, but the ashram is safe."

48

Buddhas and Bandits

Donna dispelled the rumor as lightly as she did the mosquitos, quieting my concerns. I sat with her, breathing in sweet honeysuckle as nature's night sounds momentarily soothed me before dive-bombing mosquitoes drove me to my room. I wasn't sleepy, so I pulled a book down from the shelf and laid on my bed. The compound was tranquil with only a backdrop of night-birds chirping and the thud of bugs bouncing off my window screen, but I couldn't concentrate. The words on the page meandered as my mind skittered after thoughts of Antonio. What was he doing? Was he thinking of me? Did he find our inability to be together as maddening as I did? When would the torture end?

The distant sound of feet thundering across the lawn and someone shouting fractured my fantasizing. The voice sounded like Antonio's but it was frenzied and pitched, like a scared child's. It couldn't be him. As the voice neared, the words crystallized.

"Tom. Tom. ROBBERS!"

My mind whirled as I clutched the book *How to Meditate*. Doors slammed and more shouting sliced through the silky night. Donna and Tom came out of their cottage. When their door banged shut, I crept from my cot to the door, easing it open. In the quad below, Tom and Donna stood with Antonio in a cube of yellow light that spilled from their bungalow. Tom and Donna were still dressed in the clothes I saw them in at dinner, but Antonio stood naked except for a towel knotted around his waist.

"They came over the back wall," he said, between gasps and wild gesticulations, his Italian accent thickening to a slur of syllables. "They had a weapon. I don't know maybe it was a stick. I just ran."

Hearing him say he'd fled jarred me. The pedestal I'd put him on wobbled between his cries for help and confessions of terror. I felt my love take a hit. It was his fear, fear that should be present under those circumstances, that mortalized him. He'd descended from the clouds of Dharamsala, from the side of His Holiness the Dalai Lama. Antonio wasn't allowed to be an ordinary man, in my mind.

Donna stopped halfway across the lawn, Antonio at her side, and turned toward the cottage. "TOM! ARE YOU COMING?"

I didn't hear his response, but moments later I saw his hulking figure surface and follow the two shadowy shapes into the blackness, toward the back of the compound where the bodhisattvas—monks, ex-monks, and a few Westerners seeking nirvana—stayed.

We were warned, but how did the robbers get in? The compound was surrounded by a six-foot wall embedded with shards of glass, and the front gate locked and guarded.

Tom's murky figure slipped out of sight as I heard a gunshot. Then, a fraction later, a second shot. A squall of voices roared across the compound. My heart jittered. Had Antonio been shot? I wanted to run to him but was rooted in place—my feet refused to budge.

Slivers of light slipped from the rooms around mine as others opened their doors and peered into the void; a few joined me on the balcony. I strained to hear something, but the shouting had stopped and a consuming silence descended. The stillness was so enveloping I imagined I heard the beating wings of moths seeking the light.

My eyes remained fixed on the darkness that split the compound's flowery frangipani garden from the jagged line of rugged trees. As I watched the shadows, I saw someone emerge. I stepped back into my room, unsure of who the person was. I no longer felt as brave or smug as I did sitting on Kali, listening to the police officer warn us of danger.

Donna raced into view then disappeared into the compound's clinic. Within moments, she rushed back into the darkness with armfuls of bandages and medical supplies. Soon her voice floated toward me as she re-emerged from the woods, leading a train of people. They carried two bodies wrapped in blankets on make-shift stretchers. "Please, please, please don't let it be Antonio," I pleaded to the goddesses.

As the group passed the gompa, moonlight kissed the faces of the two on the cots and I saw the kind, wrinkled face of the old chowkidar and a pilgrimaging Swiss woman. Alive, but shot. The entourage moved toward the sing-song wail of an arriving ambulance. Those of us on the balcony stayed put, watching helplessly from afar.

काली

The next day, I learned from Kansho that only a few strands of barbed wire secured the property's rear that backed onto an open field. Electricity didn't extend to that part of the property either, leaving the residents to flounder in candlelight. He'd been in his hut preparing for bed when a gang of dacoits snuck through a sagging part of the fence. Hearing shuffling feet, he cracked his door ajar. As he peeked out, four scrawny men rushed him, knocking him to the ground. One brandished a shotgun, pointing the barrel at Kansho's chest demanding money. He handed one of the bandits his wallet while the others ransacked his room, snatching items.

Kansho had little money, since monks survive on donations. As a novitiate, he'd vowed to give up worldly attachments, but there were two items from his secular life he still clung to. The bandits found what Kansho prayed they wouldn't: his camera and a pair of sturdy walking shoes his father gave him.

"They could have all the money they wanted," Kansho said, "but I couldn't let them take my camera. And, I loved the shoes even more."

When the men tried to leave with his things, Kansho rushed them and managed to grab one of the men's wiry arms. They struggled. The gunman waved his rifle. The shouting escalated, rousing the Swiss woman from her hut and the old chowkidar from his post. The two hurried toward the skirmish, the old man's flashlight bobbing in the gloom. At the sound of approaching help, the shooter whirled and fired aimlessly into the dark. A spray of homemade bullets, jagged pieces of metal, tore through the legs of both the chowkidar and the pilgrim. Kansho took the opportunity to rip the shoes and camera from the robbers as they ran into the black night.

"I thought they would kill me," Kansho said, shaking his head and looking down at his prized shoes poking out from under his mustard-colored robe. "Instead, they shot the others."

I understood his attachment. Empathized with his angst as he struggled to untangle his new identity from his possessions, remnants from his former life—his camera and shoes; my camera and journal. They were meaningless in the scheme of things, yet somehow momentous in meaning. In the months since losing and retrieving my things, I'd thought a lot about my attachments to objects. The things we carry in life don't make our worth, but the insignificances we empower them with shape us.

Kansho, a proselyte Buddhist, was also human. I wondered what I'd have done if faced with losing my camera again. Had the months and lessons from the road made me any wiser?

I recalled one of Kansho's teachings from a few days earlier, he'd said, "Everything comes from something. When slicing a sausage each slice has a piece before and after it." In other words, every event in life has something that came before it and something that comes after it. Each thought and action from the past affects our present. Each thought or action in the present affects the future.

काली

The Swiss woman's injuries were serious but her health insurance was substantial, and she was airlifted to New Delhi and then home to Switzerland. The chowkidar, an impoverished old man, couldn't afford the hospital treatments and donations to pay for his medical expenses were collected. Kansho said he didn't think the chowkidar would ever guard the ashram again. I liked the old man, he always saluted me when I rode by on Kali so I put my money into the pot, hoping enough would be raised to help him—glad he wouldn't have to sleep in a chair under a thin blanket any longer.

Some people left after the shooting, saying they felt safer in town rather than in the isolated compound. I didn't think it much mattered. Did that make me a fatalist or believer in karma? Were they the same thing? I wasn't sure. Some things I did know, I no longer saw things the same as before the shooting. The ashram was no longer a refuge for me to hide from the world; the world would find me no matter where I was. My love for Antonio drained, and the urge to run away with him no longer occupied my thoughts since seeing him panicky in a towel. He looked frail and frightened. Plus, I overheard him tell Tom one day in the dining hall, that he had a girlfriend. They'd been together for three years, but he didn't think of them as a couple. Listening to him talking about other women he'd known since leaving the monastery helped dull his sheen too. I wasn't going down that road with him.

49

Wheel of Death

"Light. Light," yelled two teens, on a scooter whipping past me.

I ignored them thinking they were warning me Kali's headlight was on even though the sun still shined. I intentionally rode with it on to make me more visible, a foreign concept in India where drivers often found the use of headlights superfluous. Their calls, however, made me conscious of Kali. Something felt amiss. For miles, I'd noticed a slight fishtailing when I stopped suddenly, but I hadn't bothered to check. Concerned, I reached back and my hand sailed across, encountering no bag. Horrified it was gone again, I pulled to the side and discovered the rack had snapped, shattering the tail light and causing the bag to hang low.

Retrieving my map, I found the nearest sizable town was about ten miles away. When I arrived, I spotted a sign depicting a gas tank and welder's torch with a gaggle of men lounging on the steps of the shuttered shop. They gazed expressionlessly at me as I pointed to the broken rack.

"Wait," said one man, ticking his head from side to side, indicating the welder would be back soon.

I dismounted, stripped off my gear, and joined the men on the steps. It was November and the days were getting colder. I wore almost all the clothes I carried. Ten, then twenty minutes passed. The men murmured among themselves from time to time, but mostly everyone sat silent. Eventually, I asked where the welder was, and one of the men was dispatched to fetch him.

The men at the welder's shop insisted I sit in a chair so I moved, leaving my saddlebag on the steps. The men didn't like that and one of them carried it over to me, giving me a sweet little smile after setting it down and backing away.

Another twenty minutes passed and still no welder appeared. "Just coming," said a new man, who joined the group. I didn't see him arrive but he knew I had and what I was waiting for. The whole town probably knew.

Forty, fifty, fifty-five, sixty minutes passed. Finally, the shopkeeper next door ambled over and with a gentle shrug of his ox-like shoulders said, "Not coming, madam." I re-strapped the bag to the precarious rack and left for Faizabad, my day's destination. I wasn't on the road long when Kali started honking and I knew the fender screws had shaken out again, and pulled over to fix it.

काली

The road buckled and the traffic thickened as I neared the city limits under soggy skies. I slowed, inhaled the pungent smells of exotic animal dung. A dozen men scrambled around in a muddy field, heaving and hoeing the poles of a Big Top tent into place. I pulled off the road and watched, the roar of caged big cats and trumpets of chained elephants fused with the crews' shouts as they jostled the poles into place. I loved the circus. My mom and grandfather took my brother and me every

Thanksgiving weekend. I loved the crackling atmosphere and romance of daring women teetering on high wires, clowns bouncing out of cars, elephants balancing on stools, and lions leaping through flaming hoops. As a kid, the aroma of fresh popcorn, spun cotton candy, grilled hotdogs, urine-soaked hay, and human tension was electric. I dreamed of being a performer and tried to "tame" our dog Bobby by teaching her to climb a ladder, using a toy rope-whip my grandfather bought me.

The cotton whip made a disappointing pfft sound as I snapped it at Bobbie, who snapped back. She wasn't one to be ordered about. I put her paws on the first rung nonetheless, but she darted away. I chased her down, but she slipped from my arms. Bobbie was an experienced jumper, always eager to follow my brother and me as we leapt out our bedroom window and ran back inside in games of chase, whenever our grandparents looked after us. But that had been her choice, and she wanted no part of the ladder or my attempts to tame her. When my mother saw Bobbie squirming on the ladder, she threatened to confiscate my whip if she caught me terrorizing the dog again.

I waited patiently in a line with others to enter the Big Tent. I found it odd, given Indians' nature for pushing and shoving, that no one crowded me. But when the gates flung open, they surged forward in the true spirit of every man, woman, and child for themselves. A guy in his twenties, in a pair of skinny black jeans, tried to shove past a little boy bundled in bright knit until I put my hand on the teen's shoulder and said, "Wait." A storm moved in his heavily lidded eyes, but I'd distracted him long enough for the little boy and his mother to slip into the tent. I'd purchased a seat on the floor and blundered my way in the dimness to the folding chairs, while families climbed several rows up to the bleacher seats. It was December 4, my mother's birthday, and I was excited to relive a piece of my childhood in honor of her. I scanned the arena. A sea of slack faces glistened in the dark, looking as if they'd come to witness a trial and not the Greatest Show on Earth.

A speaker crackled with unintelligible garble as a caged lion was wheeled into the ring. Nostalgia nipped me; the circus always made me feel that anything was possible.

A man bounded into the center wearing a speckled tie, the tails of his tux flapping behind him. He doffed his top hat at the lack-luster crowd and bowed. At first glance, he appeared as shiny and sparkly as the ringmasters of my childhood, but as he twirled and chattered into the microphone, I noticed the suit's frays and faded color. The ebony lapels looked scorched from too many pressings from a *dhobi* wallah's heavy coal-fueled iron, and many of the rhinestones in his hat were missing. I couldn't understand his words but his tone thrilled me, promising wondrous feats.

The ringmaster doubled as the lion tamer, instructing circus hands to let the lion loose. The tamer popped his whip and the lion twisted his head, emitting a puny complaint and stretching his scrawny neck to reveal a worn, tufted mane. The bob at the end of his tail was little more than wisps of fur. The lion tamer's whip forced the sorry jungle king to hop through a series of fire rings before bringing three lionesses into the act. The quartet clabbered onto each other's back, erecting a tower for the uninspired audience. I felt sorry for the majestic beasts, reduced to pacing in iron cages and forced to perform acts that neither wowed or awed the spectators. I regretted coming. My cherished childhood memories were tarnished by what I saw. Still, I couldn't look away.

Two tigers and a female assistant were added to the mix to liven the crowd. She pranced into the ring sporting a black bodysuit, green tights, blue tennis shoes, and black socks. Bowing, she threw her arms into the air urging the audience to clap. They remained stoic, and I wondered what they expected? I wondered what I expected?

After the lions and tigers came bears, elephants, horses, birds, clowns, and girls, girls, girls. They juggled, hula-hooped, trotted on balls, spun in the air by their necks, and tiptoed across high wires. They swayed on shaky ladders in ill-fitting costumes that revealed their youth. Where did they come from? Were they born into the circus or abandoned by parents too poor to afford girls and the dowries that came with them? Or had they joined the circus seeking excitement and freedom?

Most of the acts did little for the crowd, until the clowns rolled in. The audience burst to life, stamping their feet and clapping, emitting hoots and shouts as the clowns—little people except for one regular-sized boy—pulled chairs out from under each other and shot each other from cannons. The tent lights flickered with predictable power outages, and we waited for it to be restored and illuminate another act.

For the finale, a young woman strutted into the ring dressed in a red motorcycle jacket, black satin shorts, and fishnet tights. She wore her ebony hair long and loose, a pair of gold earrings glittered as she pursed her red lips and slowly turned, letting the crowd glory in her being, before swinging her leg over a motorcycle and kickstarting it to life. It wasn't a Bullet but a little Kawasaki. On it, she soared off ramps and hurdled barrels like Evil Knievel, skidding to stops and pivoting her bike—as Nanna taught me to do in tight spaces. The audience thundered its adoration, and the tent pulsed with empowerment as she revved the engine over and over.

The daredevil carried a kind of chaos that inspired me to think of the goddess Kali. The way the rider's hair snapped in her wake and motorcycle pirouetted in frenzied energy was like the goddess' dance of destruction.

The rider ramped into an enclosed iron sphere—the Wheel of Death. Quivering like a puppet from the goddess Kali's fingertips, the red-leathered woman whizzed faster and faster inside the orb, gaining velocity and defying gravity as her bike buzzed beautifully in the caged world. I envisioned sparks spitting from the pipes, as she scored double helixes on the mesh's surface.

She slowed, circling the cage's equator, as two more women on motorcycles joined her in the sphere. The trio careened around in blurry streaks, etching the shape of an atom as they crisscrossed each other's paths. The buzz of their angry engines carved through the Big Top's stifling air. The women wore no helmets, no goggles, no gloves, no protection. Their wild hair whipped and bit their bronze skin, and a desire that they feel nothing but the power of what they're doing—nothing but the power of their being—swept through me.

50

Touristing

The air turned bitter cold and heavy clouds pressed down on me. I was within 400 miles of New Delhi and stopped often and rode shorter distances, than at the beginning of my journey. It was July then, and I rose early to beat the heat and stayed on the road until dark. Now, despite wearing many layers of clothes to stay warm, the wind still found its way inside, chilling me so that hypothermia was a possibility. Bundled up, I barely managed to maneuver Kali through towns. I was subconsciously apprehensive about what I was returning to in New Delhi. Once scared to leave, now I worried about what awaited me there.

Uttar Pradesh's capital, Lucknow, had some historical sites I wanted to visit. After checking into a hotel, I stepped back out onto its broad steps to hire a taxi for sightseeing, since I wasn't eager to ride Kali around the auto-centric city. The only person in sight was a withered old man standing next to a cycle rickshaw. I found the thought of poor, scrawny men pulling fat, rich customers around distasteful, and I could never bring myself to hire one. Had I been in New York or San Francisco, it wouldn't have felt so disagreeable to be chauffeured under human power; those peddlers were enterprising.

When I'd first arrived on the Subcontinent years earlier, I'd arrogantly thought all of India's ills and their fixes seemed clear: if things were done the way Americans did things, all would be well. But India cured me of that folly. One thing was certain, the more I thought I understood the more uncertain things became.

The setting sun over mosque spires created a relief of black steeples against a cashmere pink sky, as the old rickshaw wallah hobbled over to me. Clad in a plaid lungi, singlet undershirt, with a rash of whiskers across his chin, he asked, "Madam. Rickshaw?"

Hiring a grandfather made me uncomfortable and filled me with a sense of white privilege. But to not hire him deprived him of a living. He wasn't begging, he wanted—needed—to work.

His eager expression tugged at my conscious, but I shook my head no anyway. He didn't budge. He reminded me of the old man in Ahemdabad, who'd tugged his ears and implored me to not fight with the man or the boys who harassed us that night on the bridge, and I gave in.

We arranged the time and fare for the next day. I'd dealt with taxi wallahs long enough to know they supplemented their incomes by running tourists around to every tchotchke shop and emporium that offered backsheesh—payment—for bringing potential customers. I intended to nix that notion.

"No shopping," I instructed.

"No, madam. No shopping," he repeated, bowing deeply with his hands pressed together high overhead.

"I mean it. No shopping. I only want to visit certain sites and no shops."

"Yes. Yes. Promise. No shopping."

काली

I woke the next morning to drizzly rain and red spots all over me. The bed was infested with fleas or bedbugs that chewed on me all night. I peeked out the window hoping the rickshaw wallah hadn't shown up, but saw him waiting in the street below. Not only had he arrived, he came an hour early. I dressed, ate a quick breakfast of eggs and toast in the dining room, and headed out.

"This way, madam," the man said, professionally swiping raindrops from the vinyl seat with a shabby cloth, then flourished his hands at me, urging me to climb in. A heavily patched black bonnet covered the buggy, but the misty rain still drifted in. My guide, whose name I didn't know, pumped the pedals with trembling legs toward Bara Imambara, my first destination, a sprawling congregation hall constructed in 1784 as part of a famine-relief project, while I bounced about in the back feeling like a *memsahib*.

The rig's covering was tilted to shield me from the rain but it also obscured my view. When he stopped after ten minutes, I discovered he'd brought me to a bauble shop.

"No, no, no," I whined. "I'm not buying anything."

"Yes, madam," he agreed. "No buying. Looking only. Just five minutes."

India never changed on this score. "Just looking" and "Only five minutes" were subterfuges. Once a shopkeeper had me in his store, I was trapped. While a wallah received some rupees, I'd have my time taken. Carpets piled up, bright Kashmiri paper mâché boxes presented before me, iron-forged ornaments dangled, copious artifacts endlessly flourished—teak carvings, silver jewelry, Mogul paintings, pashmina shawls, glass vases, sandalwood sculptures, silk purses, stone gods and goddesses, vests, saris, scarves. On and on the parade would go, until I bought something just to escape.

Disappointment spread across my guide's face when I refused to get out of the rickshaw. My list of places to visit—Rumi Darwaza, Lakshman Tila, Clock Tower, Jama Masjid—was long and I hoped to fit them all into one day. He reluctantly got the cycle going, struggling up and down hilly streets as I sat feeling guilty. I'd lost twenty pounds in my five months on the road, going from a thin 125 pounds to a scrawny 105 pounds. But no matter how skinny I got, I outweighed most cycle rickshaw wallahs.

My final stop for the day was Jama Masjid, the old mosque. I climbed the minaret alone, my healed knee barely bothering me, without any lecherous boys hiding in the stairwell, and looked out at an unfamiliar city. From the tower, I saw the road that would take me out of town, but not what I'd find when I got to where I was going. I was okay with that.

Back on the ground, I asked the rickshaw wallah to take me to a nice restaurant, thinking he could pick a place that paid him for bringing me.

"Yes, madam. Very nice place. Best place," he said, grinning and grunting as he got the contraption going.

51

Full Circle

The rain cleared by the next day, but the overcast skies remained most of the morning as I rode to Bareilly. I intended to ride all the way to New Delhi, but the frigid temperature and biting winds made my hands numb, making it difficult to work the controls. I slipped in behind heavy trucks every chance I got, using their bulk to block the wind. The road was smooth but it still took seven hours to ride 112 miles because of the cold. By the time I reached Bareilly darkness had fallen. I was worn out and so was Kali, parts of her no longer working—the horn and headlight.

I trolled through the lightless town on a lightless Kali, stiff with cold and utterly lost on deserted streets, hoping to stumble upon a hotel. Finally, I flagged down a man on a scooter, asking him to lead me to one. He nodded, zipped ahead leaving me in the dark, then stopped and waited until I caught up. "There," he hollered into the wind, pointing down an alley.

I peered into the pitch but saw nothing, and he motioned me to follow again. At the hotel, there wasn't any off-street parking for Kali, but that no longer mattered as much. We'd both toughened up along the way. When the man was sure I saw the place, he honked and rode off.

Christmas was two weeks off and young businessmen milled about inside the hotel's lobby, some dressed in suits and ties and others more casual. The clerk told me a convention was in town and handed me the key to the last available room.

"Someone will bring your bags, madam," he said, nodding curtly.

"They are on the motorcycle out front," I said, my purple pack dangling from my shoulder.

"Of course, madam."

I followed a room-boy down a dim hall and waited for him to unlock the door. Inside were drab bare-bone basics—a bed and dresser shoved to one side of the room with a cushioned chair and rattan table on the other side. I flopped into the chair and surveyed the room while the boy flipped on the hot-water tank in the bathroom and the television, before taking my order for a full pot of tea. I needed copious cups to cut the chill from my bones.

A second boy bustled in with my bag, as I unlaced my boots. The snowy image on the television worried him and he fiddled with the controls. Nothing. He left the room, leaving the TV roaring and returned moments later with three men—one clutched a bucket filled with tools, the second worked on the television, and the third watched them.

"Fixing, madam," said the one with the bucket.

I nodded. The man tinkered with the television for a while but failed to fix it. The waiter arrived with my tea but found the technicians fascinating, and stood in the doorway holding the tray and gawking at the men. I finally got his attention and he put the tray down.

The men trotted away and returned with another television, but they couldn't get it to work either. My room now had two defunct televisions and three men. They left and returned with a third set, that the waiter tuned to the BBC News. More men arrived and took the two dead TVs away.

Once everyone decamped, I settled into the chair to scribble in my journal, trying to capture my thoughts on my last night on the road. Moments later someone knocked at the door. Thinking it was the waiter bringing my dinner, I called, "Come in."

"Have they all gone?"

I looked up to see a stranger wearing a singlet undershirt and polyester pants at my door. His appearance didn't unnerve me as it would have in the past, when strange men boldly walked into my hotel room to have a "look" at me. Sometimes they appeared under the pretense of bringing me unrequested soap or a newspaper, other times they did so simply because they felt it was their right. I was a woman alone after all. How "proper" could I be?

A different earlier version of me would have felt threatened by this man's invasion. Another me would have been angry. Neither of those me's would have voiced her outrage by shouting, "Get out."

"I thought I saw some people over here," he said.

"They just left," I said.

He lingered, looking at me from the dim hallway, the smoke from a cigarette at his side curling in the air. His hair was tousled, and his eyes held questions.

"I have to get back to my writing," I said. "Shut the door on your way out."

He held his place for a moment, then backed out pulling the door behind him. A short time later someone knocked again, and I called, "Come in." Nothing happened. I called out again. Still, nothing happened. I went to the door and found the man in the undershirt again.

"Do you have a match?" he asked, waving an unlit cigarette.

I thought about the matches across the room I used to light the incense smoldering on the desk, contemplating if I should accommodate him.

"No," I said, sitting back down.

He hovered in the hall, looking me up and down.

"Can I talk to you?" he said.

"Nope."

"See, I'm alone over there, and I just want to come in and be your friend."

Alone is where I felt like me, the me I wanted to be. Not the me I showed the world, but the me I kept hidden from the world. The true me. The me I was now. The me I now showed him. Without a word, I stretched my leg out and toed the door shut.

काली

I hung around the hotel until late morning the next day, hoping the temperature warmed. When it didn't, I loaded Kali with stiff fingers and toes for the final 155 miles. Squares of promising blue patches punched through the sky, and New Delhi awaited me at the end of the day. In between was a ride through raw icy wind that sliced through me, threatening hypothermia.

I went inside to check the room one last time, to be sure I wasn't leaving anything behind. A reflection of myself in the mirror made me pause. I'd indulged in a full beauty treatment a few days earlier. The esthetician had tamed my feral eyebrows, thinning them into willowy arches that imprinted me with an astonished expression that seemed fitting, given all I'd been through.

Kierkegaard said, "We live forward but we understand

backward." What I knew, what hindsight taught me, was each encounter and every experience shifted and shaped me. I left New Delhi in search of fifty-one pieces of a goddess, in an attempt to make her whole again while discovering myself. Instead of finding her pieces, I left some of myself behind with those I'd met and carried parts of them away with me. Every encounter, experience, and choice I made added to the sum of who I was and who I'm still becoming. We aren't born knowing who we are, rather we unfold over time, like a flower bud opening to life's light. Born screaming and red-faced, looking like I'd been in a fight, I'd transformed from a timid girl who hugged the wall into a woman embracing life from the back of a motorcycle, on the edge of India.

In 144 days, I'd ridden 6,719 miles. The numbers represented self-reliance, independence, and something else when I tallied them. Adding up the numbers in the number of the days I rode —one plus four plus four—equaled nine, the date of my birth: January 9. Doing the same for the miles—six plus seven plus one plus nine—equaled twenty-three. My father died on January 9 on my twenty-third birthday. His sudden death sharpened my focus on life, on how short it can be and how important it was to live it on my terms. To not be held back by anyone, especially myself.

A toxic, phosphorescent sky shimmered over New Delhi. The sour, sulfuric gases from factories stung my nostrils, as hundreds of rush-hour-traffic headlights illuminated the way. I fell into a long, thick line of vehicles that stuttered and stalled on the outskirts of the capital, preventing me from seeing what lay ahead. But it didn't matter. My dad was right. I could go anywhere, do anything, be anyone I wanted.

Afterword

Less than a year after the journey ended, I did something I never imagined possible: I left Kali to Nanna's care when I returned to the United States. Her operating system didn't meet the standards imposed on motorcycles imported. It was too expensive to bring her up to spec, and she wasn't old enough to be grandfathered in. She languished in Nanna's shop for years after I left India, gathering dust and housing mice and spiders, until an Irish oil executive read about her on my blog. He wanted to buy and restore her to her original grandeur, but I resisted. I wasn't ready to let her go, even though I knew she'd only worsen if left to languish. But, she's a Royal Enfield. A Bullet. She needed to be ridden, to reign the road. I'd shifted into a new life phase and it was time to let her do the same.

Thomas Wolfe said, "We are the sum of all the moments in our lives—all that is ours is in them: we cannot escape it or conceal it." Kali was part of me, a piece of my past. I needed to physically let her go so we could both have a future. I reminded myself that while the oilman might own the machine, he would never own Kali. She was—is—always will be—a state of my mind.

Acknowledgements

The writing of a book is a solitary act supported and ushered along by many. The Indians say namaskar or namaste, which means, "The sacred in me recognizes the sacred in you." There are so many people I'm beholden to for their support, time, friendship, and encouragement. I tried to keep a list but over the years I may have forgotten some and there were many whose name I never knew. If your name is not on this list, I am deeply sorry. Your time and insights were valued and appreciated.

This book has been a long time in the making and I've been fortunate to have many people read (some tirelessly) all or parts of this book. I want to profoundly thank Anita Anand, Jan Aylsworth, Melissa Butcher, Ruth Cash-Smith, Suzanne Dobrin, Sherry Groff, Caroline Nellis, Peggy Newman, Renée Olson, Scott Saalman, Melissa Stacer, Sarah Stevens, Jane Varner, Rebecca Ward, Ginny Wiehardt, Barbie Wilson.

I'm deeply grateful to my friends Thomas Kummerow and Luise Rürup for unconditionally taking me to their home, and to Patralekha Chatterjee and Joydeep Gupta for sage advice and storing my belongings in their home, while I traversed the edge of India. While on the road, I met thousands of open-hearted Indians, whose names I didn't know or can't recall, who helped me more than I may ever fully realize.

My friend and colleague Terri Bischoff created the wonderful cover and lended her expertise in so many ways. Her talent and spirit are bar-none.

I'm indebted to Hedgebrook Writers' Retreat for the gift of a two-month writer's residency in a cabin of my own to work on this book, and to Split Rock Arts Program, New Harmony Writers Workshop, and Indiana University Writers' Conference for scholarship support. Thank you to the many inspiring and wise writing teachers I've worked with over the years: Jo Ann Beard, Tim Cahill, Stephen Dobyns, Vijay Seshadri, Brenda Wineapple, and Penny Wolfson, as well as my many wonderful cohorts in these writing courses.

Above all, I'm blessed for the support of my family: my father Arble "Bud" who inspired me to believe and my mother Dolores—the real goddess warrior of my life—who showed me how to be the woman I am today through her quiet everyday actions. She never wavered in her belief in me and this book, and it is to her that I owe the biggest debt.

Book Club Discussion Questions

1. One of the main themes in *Untethered* is the idea of pieces, as in the pieces of the goddess Kali, and how our concept of identity is developed and shaped by what we take from others and what we leave behind. How do you define identity, and how do your thoughts align with C.L.'s?

2. What role do the motorcycle Kali and the goddess Kali play in this memoir?

3. Females are central to this narrative, not only the treatment of them in India but all over the world. C.L. considers herself strong but not brave, and struggles with how to respond to the way Ahana's sister-in-law Kiara is treated. What should foreigners do when faced with oppression in other cultures?

4. The old man, who the boys harass along with C.L. on the bridge, begs her to forgive the boys and let the incident go, but she cannot. Is she justified in pursuing the man, who sheltered the boys, down a dark alley? What does she come to realize after she trips and falls?

5. How true is Nanna's statement when he tells her, "India will provide for you," and in what ways does India provide? How does this relate to question four?

6. How have your travel experiences, nationally or in other countries and cultures, shaped you?

7. What significance do you make of C.L. finding the goddess' wrist, at her first shakti peetha temple, within days of losing her bag?

8. Why does C.L. abandon her search for the shakti peetha temples?

9. After the bridge incident, C.L. is hiding herself away in a hotel when another group of children insists she join them. Why do you think she does, after having such a negative experience with the boys a few days earlier?

10. Does C.L. ever become the badass she desires? How so or why not?

11. *Untethered* is C.L.'s story of freeing herself by detaching herself from self perceptions. Did she succeed in the end?

12. C.L. says at the beginning that she does not believe in numerology, yet at the end she makes meaning of the number of days she was on the road and total miles ridden. Why do you think she did that?

13. Early in the story, C.L. loses her bag filled with items she feels represent her identity. Later, when bandits steal a novice monk's camera she understands his struggle. How has she successfully or unsuccessfully come to terms with her own

attachments?

14. As a foreign woman alone on a motorcycle, C.L. is seen as an outsider. How do her encounters with the nomadic herds women and the hijras help her understand herself?

15. What experiences and self-perceptions from your own childhood have you struggled with, and how did you overcome them?

16. What is driving C.L. when she jumps over the side of the bridge and chases the man into a dark alley? Have you ever experienced that sort of blind rage? How did it change you?

17. At what moment in the story do you feel C.L. understands herself best?

18. How do the things C.L. believes about herself help or hurt her journey in life?

19. C.L.'s father's nickname was Bud and the Hindi script for Kali also means bud, as in a flower. Discuss the significance of this dual meaning and how it relates to C.L.'s story.

20. India and its geography are one of the books characters. How do the challenges they present help C.L. achieve her ultimate goals?

Your Free Essay Is Waiting

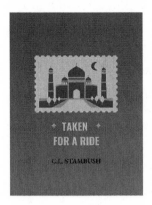

When C.L. Stambush climbed into the back of a taxi in New Delhi, India, one cold night in December, she knew the directions to her friend's house were as sketchy as a woman getting into a cab alone. But when the driver picked up his friend along the way and failed to follow her instructions, her radar went on high alert.

In *Taken for a Ride*, Stambush is forced to confront and examine who is taking whom for a ride.

Sign up for my newsletter and get your free copy of *Taken for a Ride*:

www.clstambush.com

About the Author

C.L. Stambush is a journalist, writer, and editor who has lived, worked, and traveled in more than 20 countries. Her work has appeared in the *Chicago Tribune, Cosmopolitan, Far Eastern Economic Review, Travelers' Tales*, as well as national and international newspapers. She is the recipient of awards, scholarships, and residencies from Hedgebrook Writers Colony, RopeWalk Writers Retreat, Split Rock Arts Program, and Indiana University Writers' Conference, where an early chapter from this book was judged Best Creative Nonfiction by Scott Russell Sanders.

She lived in Europe, Eastern Europe, the Middle East and Asia for six years, traveling by foot, train, truck, bus, boat, camel, donkey cart, and motorcycle. After returning to the United States, she was recruited to become a national motorcycle safety instructor where she trained hundreds of people (many of them women) to ride safely during her fourteen-year tenure.

To inquire about booking C.L. Stambush for a speaking engagement, please email hello@clstambush.com. To learn more about the author visit www.clstambush.com.

Made in the USA
Middletown, DE
12 October 2022

12620842R00168